I0112138

Dubai Catventure

Sister Feline Adventures Gone Wrong

A tail of a meowtastical sister adventure

WRITTEN BY: FIONA COLLINS

Copyright ©2024 Fiona
All rights reserved.

CONTENTS

· · ·

DEDICATIONS

. . .

As the main stars of the book and my life, I would like
to dedicate this book to Izzy and Lucia- don't be mad
at your representation, remember it is fiction. Love you
both to the moon and back.

ABOUT THE AUTHOR

. . .

After completing a Human Geography degree in the UK, Fiona transitioned to teaching. Fiona has been teaching for thirteen years which has allowed her to develop love of creativity. Every day she gets to see the power of books in the classroom and the passion children show towards literature. A favourite part of her day is reading stories to her two daughters and sharing that time together, alongside their two cats.

CHAPTER: 0.1

My name is **Izzy!**

My name is **Izzy,** *and my name is Lucia; I knew you would go first.* **Well, I am the oldest! We live in Dubai with our mum and dad and our two cats, Cleo and Caesar (this information is integral for the whole story; you'll find out soon enough).**

My name is **Lucia**

Izzy, I was going to say that part, you always get to speak before me. Anyway, just so you know, we are real people, we are really sisters, but you will find out soon that this is not a book full of facts. **Yes, some things might have been**

made up (I'm sure you will guess which parts soon enough).

It is actually our mum who will tell the story as she allegedly has a perfect memory. *She actually doesn't, but she also said that's the only way to make it fair.* **Also, she is a teacher at our school and has seen a lot of the things that happen first-hand.** *Often without us realising it.*

We might "Help" mum throughout the book if she gets anything wrong, *but don't expect to hear much from us; we are working on our listening skills at the moment.* **Well, apparently, we need to work on listening.** *I think our parents need to work on speaking clearly.*

You are expected to learn something from this book, especially if you have a sibling. *Even better if you have a sister.* **But we hope you still have fun reading it, too.** *If you don't, then it means you haven't got any taste in books.* **Lucia! You can't say that; they might think we are rude and put the book down.** *Okay, guys, sorry. All I meant was that this is a good book, so you should give it a go.*

CHAPTER: 01

'That's mine!' As Izzy screamed at her sister from the top of the stairs, she stumbled over her bemused cat, Cleo, who was innocently sleeping on the stairs. I know what you're thinking. Why would a cat be asleep on the stairs in the middle of getting ready for school? Well, that's Cleo. I'll tell you a little bit about her before we jump back into the major argument we were about to witness. Cleo is a beautiful Arabian Mau. That doesn't mean she meows a lot (even though she does). It's just a breed of cat. As she is from Dubai, it makes sense she is an Arabian Mau, as Dubai is an Arab city.

When you look at Cleo, you would think she had been splattered with paint – just white, brown and black paint. Not exactly the most vibrant colours, but it does make her a stunning cat. Now, something else you need to know about Cleo is that she is an independent woman (in the words of Beyonce). Hence, that is why she was asleep in the middle of the stairs instead of the many cat beds littered around the villa. Other people think she is a typical cat, aloof and rude, but Cleo saves all her love and affection for her family. She's not like a dog (by the way, there are no dogs in this story, so if you like dogs, maybe get a Paw Patrol book) who gets excited over seeing anyone, even the delivery guy. She is very particular; some may say fussy, but if you get a nuzzle from Cleo, you know you have earned it!

Cleo arrived in the house as a tiny bundle of a kitten during the

the Lockdown. The girls' dad, Paul, had been told there were some stray kittens in someone's garden who needed a home. Now Paul is and always will be a dog person (you're either a dog person, a cat person or just animal crazy and love them all), so when he brought Cleo home as a surprise, it sure was a big surprise! Her small, cute colourful face melted his heart, and he has had a soft spot for her ever since, even when she does poo in the tomato plant pot!

(Now, back to the argument) …

"Lucia, you knew that was the pair of socks that I had left out for my uniform. Now I am going to be running late for netball."
"These are a hundred million per cent my socks. Look, they even have the pink paint stain from my art exhibition last week!"

"Ewww, do you not even clean your socks? That's gross." With a look of disgust that was equivalent to eating a live, giant maggot, Izzy tossed the sock back in Lucia's face (quite a good aim, actually, so it was good practise for netball).

"Mum! Izzy is being mean to me." Lucia wiped the sock off her face and stared at Izzy with disdain.

Now, this could have been any morning in the Collins household (except some mornings Izzy has piano and not netball). The point is it was not a peaceful start to the day. It is never a peaceful start to the day. This is how Izzy and Lucia's mum would like to start the day in an ideal world....

"Good morning, Mother. You look radiant today! Izzy and I have a spare pair of socks for you. Would you like to wear them?" Lucia floats down the stairs with an angelic look on her face.

"Oh Lucia, my darling sister, you are so kind. What would I do without you? Mother, I am ready 20 minutes early to get into the car for school, so you don't need to ask us 5,000 times to get into the car."

"Girls have you-"

'Of course, mother, I have my piano books, netball dress, homework – completed early – and my lunch box. It looks delicious today, by the way.' Izzy carried all her bags and even her mum's handbag into the car for good measure.

.... Back to reality. Instead of the ideal morning, the arguments continued while everyone was trying to pack up the car with the mountain of different items needed for a day in a Dubai school. 'Why are you climbing over my side?'

'Does it even matter?'

'But you are getting your sandy shoes on my seat.'

SLAP!

'Mum! Izzy hit me!' Luckily, Caesar popped his head into the garage to lend a bit of light relief. Now, Caesar is the second cat in the Collins' house and is totally different to Cleo. Though they both have ancient names (Cleo, the Queen of Egypt and Julius Caesar, the ruler of the Roman empire. Actually, Cleopatra and Caesar got together in the olden days, but the cat version is brother and sister), that is where the resemblance stops. Caesar is a Scottish fold cat, which is unusual as he also lives in Dubai, but he was delivered to the house by Santa a few years ago, so his heritage is a bit of a mystery. He is definitely the wild one out of the two. His fiery orange coat reflects his nature, and he is always causing mischief in the house and around the local street. Caesar thinks of himself as the big boss of the cats, but as soon as Cleo walks in, he soon knows his place. Now, Caesar is well known for starting a fight or two (or twelve), but when it comes to the family, he's a big softie. As soon as Izzy and Lucia's dad opens his laptop to work (or to watch football), Caesar will be there straight away, ready for some well-needed attention. He will widen his green eyes so he looks like a cuddly toy that you can't resist buying from the shop and curl up around you. Within seconds, you are under his spell, and any form of work (or watching) has stopped, and you are giving him hugs and kisses.

The day Caesar arrived was the best day ever! *I know! Do you remember when we opened our presents on Christmas day, and there was that strange note under the tree?* **Yes, I had to read it, didn't I, because you couldn't read yet.** *Well, I was only 5, and the handwriting was terrible.* **I don't suppose Santa learned how to do cursive writing at the North Pole. The note said there was something we wanted, called Caesar, in the house.** *We ran around like crazy, didn't we, until we opened the spare room and there he was, the tiny little ginger kitten.* **My heart literally stopped. He was so cute!** *And remember his tiny meow? He was so quiet compared to Cleo. Do you remember I scooped him up and cuddled him too tight?* **Aww, I love Caesar. And I love Cleo, too.**

This morning, he had decided to get into the car and nearly had a field trip to school. All three humans were scrambling around the car, chasing him back into the house, flapping around like headless chickens. Caesar did enjoy the chaos as he hid under the car, then on the roof and finally, he sauntered back into the house as if nothing had happened, shaking his ginger bottom as he swaggered past Cleo, wondering what all the fuss was about. And this was only ten past six in the morning!

Let's rewind about two years, and this would have been a very different scene. Izzy and Lucia were inseparable. They would play with their Barbies for hours together, creating new and wonderful adventures for them to go on. Even Caesar and Cleo were forced into their games and became 'rides' for the Barbies to travel on or forced into the pram for a walk around the house in the 'babysitter game'. They would go to the pool together all the time and splash each other and play police in the pool until they were practically dragged out of the water (Cleo and Caesar would take a synchronised sigh of relief as the girls went to the pool – one place you will never find a cat). When they both got scooters, they would beg their parents to pack them up into the car so they could scoot together, chatting and giggling down the boulevard at Kite Beach or around the different pavilions at the Expo. Lucia would always be so busy chatting to Izzy that she would often bump into the rollerbladers and the joggers, spraying sweat everywhere. One time, someone was so shocked by Lucia spinning towards them that they ran straight off the path, and their face collided with the sand. As they spat the sand out of their shocked mouth and mixed sweat and sand together in a weird cement mixture, the Collins family sped up quickly in the direction of the car with embarrassed looks on their faces. But as the years drifted by, Izzy and Lucia's playing became less and less, and the arguments became more and more regular.

As the girls arrived at school, they had had more fights than Mike Tyson. Now, for those of you who have no idea about boxing, you'd be the same as me. However, one person I do know is Mike Tyson, and I know he can pack a strong punch. (Paul has informed me there are at least five more famous boxers in 2024, but I'm sticking with this simile.) This did not mean the girls were physically fighting, though they were tugging on their mum's patience. Their version of fighting was with their viper tongues. Like a snake, they would throw poison at each other the whole way to school – and with Dubai traffic, this could be a painful journey. A rainbow of vehicles would pile up on the busy roads, and their car would get slower and slower the closer they got to school. Round after round of arguing, which would often end in their mum (the referee) turning the radio off before the Virgin Radio Pop Quiz and making them sit in silence. This would really aggravate them as they wanted to know if the lucky contestant had won the 10K prize (the girls' mum always thought she would win it and screamed out the answers, but she's never rung in to prove it).

Getting into school wasn't much better. As they pulled up to the towering school building, they continued to glare at each other. The sunlight shone off the iridescent glass, inviting the children in. This was a very different school to the one the girls' mum had gone to in England. The bushes lined the entrance like the promenade to Buckingham Palace. Okay, it wasn't that grand, but the four-storey building stood proudly ready for the school day. Today was Izzy's turn to use the security tag to open the sensor doors, but that did not end the other disagreements to come. Both of them needed to open the door first, both of them needed to go up the stairs first, and both of them needed to say bye to their mum first. Of course, you can only have one first place, and there is always a second place, but when it comes to sibling rivalry, there is no shaking of hands like the end of a tennis match. It is glaring and shouting.

Once they had separated and finally made their way to their own separate classrooms, there was peace within the bustling corridors.

Today, we will follow a day in the life of Izzy. Sometimes, it is easier to start with Izzy as she is the eldest. Right now, she is nearly ten years old and in Grade 4. This means she has the attitude of a teenager but still wants to play with her toys, so her mind is constantly filled with happiness and conflict. Izzy has dark blonde hair and freckles sprinkled across her face. When she smiles, she can light up the room (you just have to wait a little longer for that smile to happen now she's nine). Her dry sense of humour can mask how caring she is as kindness runs through her body like oxygen. She loves to read, and she used to read books to Lucia every night when she was supposed to be in bed. She thought I couldn't hear her sneak into Lucia's room to read her another story, but I didn't mind as they were being nice to each other.

With the flick of her thick hair, she is merged into her friendship group with enough sass to fill a whole Instagram page. The gaggle of her and her friends echoed around the corridor and into the classroom, where her teacher was patiently waiting for the girls to finish their gossiping and return inside.

Now, this is where Mum is going to start making things up. She knows my friends and my teacher, but she feels it "isn't fair" to put them into the book without their permission. I told her they would be cool with it, but as ever, she is "always right". So, this means the people who are being described aren't my real teacher or my friends; it is very much from my mum's imagination. So good luck with that!

"Izzy, time to get inside. We actually have some learning to do apart from who watched the latest video from Mr Beast." Mr Baldy ushered the girls inside, waving his arms around like he was a helicopter about to take off. Mr Baldy was one of those teachers who told a million dad jokes an hour, but because he was kind and always listened to every single girl drama in the class, they would laugh along with him or give him a cheeky roll of their eyes with a grin attached. He towered over the Grade 4s like a giant stomping around the school. Is it a coincidence his name is Mr Baldy? Absolutely not. His bald head shone in the Dubai sun and reminded the girls of a bowling ball about to hit a strike. This made him look even more like a fairy tale villain, and the younger grades would avoid him as he rumbled through the corridor. When the girls first joined his class, they were quivering behind their desks as his voice boomed around the classroom. But they soon realised that the only boom coming from his classroom was the joke about his cousin selling fireworks – business was booming! But of course, the class didn't tell the younger grades about his kind nature and would let them quiver in fear as he took his coffee mug back to the staffroom while they giggled at their ignorance.

"Woah, Sir, did you actually see it?" Izzy and her friends suddenly thought their teacher might be the coolest adult they knew.

"Of course, I didn't. I have no time to watch YouTube when I have homework to grade. Talking of homework, where was yours, Izzy?" As quickly as the excitement started, the bubble soon burst, and the girls sighed as only pre-teen girls can – with a huge amount of melodrama.

"Mr Baldy, I honestly was going to do my homework. It was just too hard. Could we not do more writing, science, unit, moral, anything but maths!" This was a familiar excuse for Izzy. Where she exudes confidence amongst her friends, give her a piece of maths to do and it's as if her brain has started oozing out of both of her ears. So, instead of doing her maths homework, she imagines this grey mushy stuff, which she assumes is her brain, dribbling down her jawline and onto the piece of paper filled with maths equations.

She slumps herself on her desk, hiding from Mr Baldy's disappointed face. She wanted to be like her best friend, Fatima. She always did her maths homework in 5 seconds (well, Izzy felt like it was 5 seconds, but it was probably longer). Fatima would often ask for more complex problems because she found the maths too easy. She always offered to help Izzy, but this would make Izzy's brain splurge even more. Fatima was one month younger than Izzy. How was she so much better than her?

"Izzy, I've told you so many times." Started Mr Baldy.

"Yes, I know, 'if I let the problem scare me, I will never be able to do it." Izzy had heard this speech before.

"But I'm right. You are more than capable. You just need to get over the fear." Izzy had already switched off and was staring at the construction outside the classroom window. Living in Dubai, you were never too far away from a new building being built and outside her school was no exception.

Now, don't get me wrong, Izzy loved going to school, especially her school. Though the building was a huge glass maze, she loved the feeling she had when she was there. When she first arrived at the school, she thought she would never learn which direction to go in for all her classes. There were so many corridors, all with different inspirational phrases, that she couldn't read. But as she grew up, she was mesmerised by the sound of shuffling feet up and down the many stairs, and she would often stare at the many portraits of old Headmistresses that lined the walls. I mean, a little maths was not going to stop Izzy from enjoying her time at school. But one thing could – bumping into her sister!

As Grade 4 left the scorching playground after a long but fun break, Grade 1 entered for their time to play on the floating playground. Now, the playground didn't actually float. It was on the first floor above the square and looked out onto the many skyscrapers that twinkled across the skyline. Each time the sunlight hit the reflective glass of a building, a new light show was produced. This is why the children liked it so much (also because they wanted to see how high they could get the squishy balls before they went over the edge towards the staff car park below). Usually, Izzy and Lucia didn't see each other at school as they spent time with their friends. But this day, their paths crossed, and all it took was a roll of the eyes from Izzy and a tongue out from Lucia to start World War Three.

All of a sudden, they were face to face, shouting at each other while a small crowd gathered around.

'You're so embarrassing, Lucia!' shouted Izzy.

'You're the one shouting at a Grade 1; now that's embarrassing!'

'GRRRR!'

Now, this is not making the girls look particularly well-behaved, and that isn't true. Individually, both girls were good students and keen role models at school. The only problem is they knew exactly how to wind each other up. This is why it only took one stern look from Mr Baldy to encourage Izzy inside to continue with the rest of her day.

'She is so annoying!' Izzy slammed her maths homework book (still empty) into her locker and let out an exacerbated sigh that blew her fringe high into the air.

'Who?' replied Fatima, loading her locker with extra maths exercises from her teacher that kept spilling out like a volcano.
'My sister, I mean, I don't see why she has to come to this school.'

'Aww, I think she is cute.'

'That's the thing, everyone thinks she is cute, but they don't see what she's really like.' The girls packed up their things and joined the mob of children making their way to Spanish. Fatima had always had a little soft spot for Lucia, but she didn't have any siblings, so she didn't realise the love-hate relationship that came with another person sharing nearly every aspect of your life.

Hang on, this whole bit is about Izzy. Why haven't you mentioned anything about my class and my day?

I knew this would happen, but I didn't think it would happen this soon!

Lucia also loves school, but not for the same reasons as Izzy. Breaktime is Lucia's time to shine. She relishes the chance to be with her group of friends and play all sorts of different games. For Izzy, the whistle means returning to new learning and exciting questions. For Lucia, it means the end of fun and back to reality. Lucia is blonder than Izzy and loves to swish her long hair about like a 'my little pony'. Her blue, gleaming eyes are always smiling from the inside, and she is well aware of how to flutter her eyelashes to get something she wants. Lucia is still a few years off the pre-teen attitude but is still close to the toddler tantrums of her past. Though Lucia loves things (she will literally steal from the crown jewels for a piece of chocolate), her heart is overflowing with love, sometimes too much love, and she won't stop giving you kisses and cuddles before bed or squeezing Cleo and Caesar in a tight bear hug.

"I can't believe break is over already." Lucia sighed and picked up her bag, trailing behind everyone else in the line.

"Lucia, you always say this! break is the same length every day." Her friend Liliana linked arms with her, then Cora joined Felicity, and they finally joined the rest of their line.

Mum said the same for me. She knows all of my friends and has even taught some of them, so she has used her imagination to change them. I said my friends love books but she wouldn't listen. I guess she did the same for Izzy, so it's fair.

When they returned to their Grade 1 classroom, Lucia could already see the writing books set out on the table. She let out another huge sigh (I don't know where she gets all the air to have this many sighs).

"Mr Jackson," Lucia raised her hand, "can we work with our friends today?" Lucia already knew the answer, as she had asked this question many times before. When Lucia worked in a group, she shone. She had innovative ideas, she listened to others, and she was a creative mastermind. However, when she had to work on her own, distractions got the better of her. Mr Jackson was not going to be outsmarted by a Grade 1 student trying to get out of work. In his spare time, he creates new educational apps for the kids to trial at home. If his brain was visible, you would see it whirring away like a bustling factory, every millimetre of it working overtime. Though Mr Jackson's shaggy hair often covers most of his eyes, he is always aware of everything happening in the classroom. It is as if he is in one of those CCTV rooms – the ones with all the small black and white cameras in.

"No, Lucia, this is an independent writing task today." Mr Jackson passed her a new pencil, so she had no excuse to go and sharpen it. But Lucia wasn't going to be put off that easily.

Step 1:

"Mr Jackson, I need the toilet." Lucia tried her luck.

"You just had break."

Step 2:

"Mr Jackson, I hurt my little finger on the playground. I should probably go to the nurse."

"Let me look, hmm…shall I cut it off?" Now, for anyone reading this and who is in a school, this is a classic teacher line to get children to not fuss about their injury. Mr Jackson, of course, was not going to chop her finger off. No children were harmed in the making of this book.

"No!"

"Right, well, you will be fine." Lucia gave up and sat down. She stared out the window at the view of the construction outside. She tried to see if she could squint and see the Burj Khalifa in the distance. Their school had four floors, and this year, she was promoted to the first floor! This meant she had a much better view of what was going on outside. The entire school was like one colossal window; each classroom had a whole wall of ceiling-to-floor glass to let the sunlight in. This was quite annoying when they were trying to look at the difference between light and dark, but the rest of the time, it meant they always knew the sun was shining. Except today, Lucia could see grey clouds beginning to bubble in the distance.

"Lucia?"

"Yes...?" Lucia came out of her trance and looked at Mr Jackson. "Time to get on."

Now, I feel I have evenly given you an insight into the Collins girls' day at school. Both girls thrive in their own way. Izzy loves questioning every little detail. Her curiosity has no limits. From when she was two, she would be baffled by different scientific questions such as, 'Why do we have saliva in our mouths,' to, 'Why does a rainbow start with red,' and sometimes the questions were just crazy, 'Why can't a whale live in the bath?' Lucia brings her optimism to everything she does. Lucia doesn't walk; she skips. Lucia doesn't talk; she sings. Lucia doesn't just smile; she howls with laughter.

The problem is, when these two forces of nature are put together, just like hot air and cold air, it can form a hurricane. And that is exactly what happened when they got home.

The sound of bellows reverberated around the house like a bomb going off. Both Caesar and Cleo scarpered in different directions to escape the upcoming combat. Get your popcorn; the battle is about to begin...

'Lucia has been in my room!' Strike one from Izzy. She was standing at her desk after throwing the first grenade into the battle.

'No, I haven't. You are always accusing me of doing something I haven't.' Strike two from Lucia as she stormed into Izzy's room to launch her counterattack.

'You're in here right now!' Strike three. An easy one from Izzy as Lucia has walked straight into her trap.

'MUM, Izzy is trying to trick me!' Strike four is a classic. Get Mum involved to try and get an ally on side.

I won't go into how many different strikes there were on this occasion, as I feel you have gotten the idea. Needless to say, this ended up with both girls not pre-empting the final and most devastating strike on both of them. Their Dad.

Now, Paul is a calm, fun character and has the patience of a saint. But even he was pushed to join the battle by this point. He is a footballer at heart and believes in a good fair game, but if you go offside, he is not happy about it, and at this point, both girls were well and truly offside! His love for both girls would stretch past the desert. Actually, it would stretch to the moon and back. Actually... well, you get it. He would do anything for Izzy and Lucia, but the sound of them arguing was like nails on a blackboard (for those of you born after the year 2000, a blackboard is, well, a black... board and you use chalk on it to write, this is how people had to learn in the olden days before iPad and smartboards and THE INTERNET).

'BOTH OF YOU DOWN HERE NOW!' Izzy and Lucia slunk down the stairs, again stumbling over Cleo, who had decided the fight might go on for a while and went to sleep on the top step. However, her curiosity got the better of her, and she followed the girls and crept down the stairs alongside Caesar, who has just come from Lucia's room after having a fight with a beanie baby toy and losing.

'I am sick of your fighting. Look at Cleo and Caesar; they are siblings, and they don't fight all the time. Both of you can go to your rooms.' Caesar and Cleo both look up expectantly at the sounds of their names. They think this either means food or time for a cuddle. Then they look at Paul's facial expression and decide it's neither of those options and begin to clean themselves.

The girls looked at each other with disdain and stomped up the stairs in the only way children can when they have realised they were in the wrong. In unison, they both fling themselves onto their beds in their separate rooms with a huff and a puff that would blow the house down (oh, sorry, that's a different story).

In Dubai, it hardly ever rains. I mean, it is a desert, so most of the time, it is bright sunlight and blazing heat, but that night, it was like Izzy and Lucia had annoyed the clouds so much a storm had begun. The rain splattered against the windows, and the thunder rumbled in the distance.

"What is dad on about?" Izzy wondered to herself. Cleo snuggled up to Izzy to shelter away from the wind and the rain outside. There was no way she was going out until the weather had calmed down and returned to the radiant sunshine Cleo was acclimatised to.

"He makes no sense." Lucia thought in her head. Caesar climbed onto her bed and got himself comfortable. There was no way he was going outside to fight with the local cats when the lightning would give away his hiding spots.

"We are not cats." Izzy began to tuck herself into bed.

"If we were Cleo and Caesar, it would be easy." Lucia's eyes began to flutter asleep as a huge bolt of lightning illuminated the villa. Little did they know what they had just done.

CHAPTER: 02

The next day, normality had resumed, ready for the weekend. The sky had cleared and had left room for the sun to blaze into the Collins' villa. It was going to be yet another glorious day. You would never even know it had been raining; the sun was like a road cleaner and somehow evaporated a whole storm of water from the roads. This was lucky as the Collins family had fun weekend plans for today.

'Girls! Come on, it's time for breakfast.' Izzy slowly blinked her eyes open at the sound of her mum's voice and stretched herself awake. She gazed around her bedroom as she normally did, noticing the clothes left on the floor from the day before and the curtain slightly ajar, letting in the scorching light. But when she stretched, her eyes bounced open as she wasn't just stretching her arms and legs; she suddenly noticed she was stretching a tail! Not just any tail, a brown, black and white splodged tail. She stared at her hands, but she couldn't see her hands; she saw a furry paw and then another one, and another one AND ANOTHER ONE. She blinked again to wake herself up properly, but when she did, her eyesight, amazing eyesight, couldn't help but stare at her now furry, multi-coloured body.

In the next room, Lucia was still snoring peacefully. Her cuddly toys were scattered across her bed as if they'd been to a late-night party. The position they had got themselves into looked like a whole load of trouble. There was Julie the monkey, with its leg wrapped around Bella the Stingray. Ollie the Oryx wasn't much better as he must have landed on top of the mouse toy in the night, squishing it at the end of the bed. Lucia's ears twitched at the sound of a voice in the distance; she kicked her legs out of bed but felt the cold chill of the tiles. Why was she on the floor? As she woke up, she went to stand up but realised she wasn't standing on two feet. She was standing on four!

Next door, Izzy was trying not to panic but was failing! She was circling round and round on the floor, moving her head in each direction to survey the familiar but strange body, tail swishing violently behind her. Lucia nudged Izzy's bedroom door with her nose. She had no idea why she did this, but she needed to find Izzy. The only problem was all she could see was Cleo. "Izzy, Izzy, I need your help. Where are you?" Lucia couldn't see Izzy anywhere but spotted Cleo circling the floor manically.

"Lucia, don't freak out, but…" Lucia and Izzy both froze, staring at each other. But it wasn't each other. It was their beloved cats, Cleo and Caesar.

The girls, well, the cats, began to sniff at each other.

"Why are you sniffing me?" Izzy lifted her paw and batted Lucia away.

"You were sniffing me!" Lucia replied.

"I know. I mean, I don't know why. I just felt like I should. My room really stinks!"

Mum, don't say that. People might think my room really does smell, not that I now have super cat-smelling abilities.

Both girls jolted into Izzy's bathroom and jumped onto the sink cabinet to survey themselves in the mirror. Izzy could see long brittle whiskers growing out of her furry head, and she rotated her ears, one black and the other brown and white. She continued to look and saw the cute little pink nose sniffing around her surroundings. Lucia also stood in shock at what she saw. Ginger, stripy fur covered her body, a little round tummy hung under her which wasn't there before, a tail swishing behind her.

Izzy's nose twitched, and her whiskers rippled. Confusion was suffocating the room. After a while, Izzy and Lucia began to look each other up and down with more focus. Lucia's green crescent eyes were razor sharp, and she was looking at Izzy's room from a much lower perspective. If they weren't in such shock, they would have realised they could find multitude of lost toys under Izzy's bed that is only visible from a cat's perspective. Lucia's ginger fur bristled with the sound of every car driving past.

Izzy's triangular ears also heard the cars in the distance, and they swivelled on the top of her furry head. She tested her new four legs by springing onto her chair with perfect precision.

"We need to go and tell Mum and Dad what's happened." Lucia used her new sense of smell to realise that they were downstairs in the kitchen. "They'll know what to do."

"Yes, because their kids turning into cats is a usual problem for them to handle." Izzy sneered sarcastically but trotted after Lucia down the stairs with a new rapid speed. Lucia turned around to argue back to Izzy but burst out laughing.

"What are you doing?!" Izzy had stopped and sat down mid-way down the stairs with her hind legs stretched into the air, her tongue licking her back leg.

"I don't know. I just had to clean my leg. It felt like it wasn't clean, but look at my flexibility! Coach Amy would be amazed at this." Her cat leg was nearly behind her head; Izzy had forgotten how flexible cats can be.

"This is no time for gymnastics, Izzy! We need to get downstairs quick; I can hear Dad getting the car keys out." Lucia twitched her ears. "I can't believe how well I can hear now." Both girls... cats... well, Izzy and Lucia, continued down the stairs and trotted into the kitchen, gathering around their parents. Only problem is they were only 50 cm tall!

"Mum, Mum, Mum, help us please, something crazy has happened. I'm in Cleo's body, and Lucia is in Caesar's body... Mum, Mum, MUM!"

Now, usually, this sort of shouting would cause a mass panic around the house. I mean, they have turned into cats! This is a serious situation. But this is what everyone else heard.
"Meow, Meow, Meow, meow, meeeeeooooooow."

"What is wrong with these cats this morning? Did you feed them?" Paul opened the fridge and poured some cat food into their bowls. "Here you go. That should keep you quiet."

"DAD, you've got to listen! It's us, Izzy and Lucia. DAD!"

"Silly cats," Paul picked up Cleo (remember this is Izzy) and plonked her in front of the cat bowl. He then did the same to Caesar (Lucia).

Both of the girls took one sniff of the meaty, gravy, FISHY cat food and nearly threw up in the bowls. The greyish, brown chunks

34

looked like poo-coloured jelly and didn't smell much better either. "He's got to be kidding," Izzy said, "I'm not eating that! It looks disgusting."

"Smells it, too! Come on, they're heading to the car." Izzy and Lucia followed their parents out to the garage and were stunned into silence.

What they saw made total sense... and no sense at all.

Two girls were sat in the back of the car, seat belts on. But these weren't two random girls. They were Izzy and Lucia. All of a sudden, 'Lucia' licked 'Izzy's' face and rubbed her cheek up against her. Izzy (in Cleo's body) had a bolt of realisation (you might've figured it out, too, but Lucia can sometimes be distracted from the obvious).

"Lucia, if we are in the cats' bodies.... The cats must be in our bodies! And they're about to drive away with our parents!"

CHAPTER: 03

As Paul clambered into the driver's seat, Lucia took the opportunity to use her new cat skills to jump into the car, nearly scaring Paul half to death. He jumped what looked like a metre out of his seat and slammed his feet on the pedals- even though he hadn't started driving yet.

"Get out, Caesar! These cats must've been spooked by the storm last night. They're going wild." He turned around to look at the two human girls sitting in the back in silence. "In comparison to the girls who are super chilled this morning." As Paul threw Lucia out of the car (luckily, her cat skills helped her land on her feet), he closed the car door and revved the engine loudly. As the car reversed out of the garage and onto the dusty road, all Izzy and Lucia could do was watch, from a very low height, their parents, their car, and their BODIES drive away into the distance. There was no way a cat, or two cats, could keep up with the speed of a car, especially when Paul was driving.

While Izzy stared at the now empty road, questions and worry whirled around in her brain. Lucia sauntered back into the house with swag, twisting and shaking her bum in the air.

"Where are you going?" Izzy shouted at Lucia, who was already leaping onto the sofa and stretching her back in a perfect U shape.

"Have you ever thought how lucky the cats are, no school, no chores, no nagging from mum and dad? They can just laze around the house all day, and we look after them," she took another huge stretch and yawned, showing off her jagged canine teeth, "Let's take some time to reeeelax."

"Are you mad!?" Izzy jumped alongside Lucia and batted her with her blotchy paw, "We can't just stay as cats! What about our whole life? This is ridiculous."

"Come on, Izzy, what can we do? Our bodies have driven off with Mum and Dad."

"UGH Lucia, you can't just sleep. This is an EMERGENCY!" as Lucia curled up on the now gigantic sofa, Izzy paced up and down, swishing her tail erratically. Her eyes were glowing green with anger towards Lucia.

"This is typical of you, Lucia. You don't take anything seriously." "Typical me! Typical you! You are always moaning, moan, moan, moan." Lucia let out a catty growl at Izzy, embracing her inner cat.

Now, luckily for Lucia, Izzy is always questioning and thinking analytically. Even though Izzy was in a cat body, her human brain was working overtime. All the questions of the morning circled around in her head: what was different yesterday? Why had they switched? What had they done? Where had her parents gone with her, HER body? While Izzy was spiralling into her thought process, Lucia was beginning to settle into the life of a cat. She had walked in a circle, over and over again, until she found the optimum spot to take a nap. Once she had her nap, she felt like her fur was covered in dirt, and she had the sudden urge to lick herself everywhere. As she licked her paw and rubbed it over her head, she began to think about what she was doing. She was licking her body; her tongue was getting furry and dry. The next place to clean was her paws, and she thought about where she had seen Caesar wandering about with the same feet over the last few days. She was pretty sure Caesar had stepped in dog poo that some naughty person hadn't cleaned up. She soon realised this was one step too far.

'Izzy, she shouted.' Izzy came trotting in and leapt up next to Lucia, 'We have got to do something.'

'Lucia, I have been thinking about this for hours. You're slow on the uptake.'

'Okay, Okay, well, what bright ideas have you had?'

'I think we need to go to Fatima and tell her, she's my best friend.'

'No way! She's too obsessed with her work. She'll never believe this is happening. I think we should go to Liliana's house, but let's go later when we kn-'

'Don't even suggest it.'

'Fine, well, I will wait here. You go to Fatima's. Then we'll see who gets this situation sorted.'

'Fine!' Izzy felt another sister fight beginning to brew, and she had no time to give it.

Lucia and Izzy jumped down in unison and trotted in opposite directions, Lucia towards the stairs and up to the bed and Izzy towards the vast street. They both suddenly realised the magnitude of what they had taken on, but their stubbornness forced them to put each of their four feet in the opposite direction in search of some support.

CHAPTER: 04

'Dance for me dance for me dance for me oh uh.' Fatima was singing as she started getting ready. She had completed all her homework and was excited to head to Dubai Mall to spend some of her birthday money. She had realised if she saved her money, she would wait for the exchange rate to improve so she could spend more money.

See, I told you, she's a genius. Always thinking of maths!

Izzy and Fatima had been friends since Izzy had joined her school. Unfortunately for Izzy, she joined a brand new school in the middle of lockdown and had to start a brand new class wearing a mask and sitting at an isolated table – not exactly the best way to make new friends! One point five metres away from her was Fatima, who had just moved from Egypt and wore the most colourful, vibrant mask.

'I like your mask.' Izzy braved to say.

'Thanks, I thought I'd try and make this situation a little bit brighter.'

'I had the same idea.' Izzy lifted out her individual pencil case (as you couldn't possibly share any resources in 2020). It was just as bright and shimmering as Fatima's mask. What they both didn't realise was that they were grinning under their masks, and their friendship began.

While Fatima got ready in her apartment, staring out at the

skyline of Dubai, Izzy was slowly, VERY slowly making her way in her direction. Now Fatima was five minutes away from Izzy's house in the car, but cats are not the same speed as a car, so Izzy had to think outside the box. Since Izzy had left the house, she had been strategising. Trotting along the path, Izzy took in her familiar surroundings from a cat's perspective. In Dubai, one thing you can always find on the road is vans. People are always ordering new things and moving house, so there are thousands of open-back vans driving around the bustling city. Izzy took this opportunity; once she had crept towards the main road and avoided the rapidly speeding cars, she kept her astute eyes open, ready to pounce on a van.

Now I know what you're thinking (and if you weren't thinking it, you should have been). How did Izzy know where the van was going? She could end up in a van going all the way to Sharjah, and she would be scuppered. Being stuck in the middle of Sharjah was not an option. Getting in and out of Sharjah was a daily quest for drivers. Sharjah was the neighbouring Emirate, and there was always hectic traffic there. But she was more intelligent than that. She knew that if the van was in the far-left lane, it would be doing a U-turn. If it was doing a U-turn, that would get her close enough to Fatima's apartment building to save some precious time. The only problem was that the only van she found in the far left lane was a van with very unusual passengers. The van was filled with scruffy, stinky, spitting camels! They huffed and puffed next to each other and grunted at every single bump in the road. So, sitting there on the side of the dusty road, Izzy had a decision. Keep wasting precious time waiting for another van or buddy up with a herd of camels.

It is actually a caravan of camels because they are used for transport. I know this because I am in the Camels Class. All the classes have animal names. Izzy is an Arabian Wolf.

With a colossal pounce, Izzy soared through the stifling air and slap bang into a... Yep, you guessed it. A massive pile of camel poo.

"UGH!" Izzy began to wipe the rotten poo from her whiskers. She slithered and snaked to a shadowed corner of the van away from the putrid camels. Under the belly of a fuzzy, fat camel, Izzy tried not to use her heightened sense of smell to whiff the 'fragrant' farts that whoffed into her face. It was surprising that camels smelled so bad when they only ate grass and leaves, but Izzy definitely didn't feel like she was in a garden. Each time the van went over a bump, the hooves of the camels came worryingly close to Izzy. As she was now in a cat's body, she was much more vulnerable to an injury from a camel. I mean, even in her human body, a camel could probably do a lot of damage if it was running fast enough. Izzy applied her cat skills to play a game of dodge the camel with their feet (and don't forget each camel has four huge hooves).

Bump. Izzy hops to the left.

Bump, she swerves right, away from a roaming hoof.

Bump. It was like she was doing a strange cat rhythmic dance. Finally, after what felt like an eternity, the van took the U-turn – which forced a camel's hoof straight onto Izzy's tail – and she could finally see the familiar building in front of her. The brand was clearly spelt out in glittering metallic letters. Izzy waited patiently for the red light and dived out of the van and onto the pavement. Shining like the sun, the glass exterior building suddenly looked a lot larger than Izzy remembered. Things often look much bigger for a cat than a human, but Izzy had no choice. Sneaking as stealthily as a… as a…. as a… cat, she squeezed and slid past the crowds of people, making their way into the foyer, where she was faced with her next challenge. The elevator!

She had managed to sneak past the throngs of people into the foyer as she was small, and the foyer was busy with people going to business meetings and nannies pulling wailing toddlers. However, an elevator was another matter. Cats are certainly not allowed in an elevator, and it was an extremely small space to try and hide – even for a cat.

This left Izzy with one choice. The fire exit light was beckoning her over. With a huge sigh, Izzy scampered towards the open door and the mountain of stairs. Surprisingly, it was easier than she thought. Cat energy is much better than hers – it must be all the naps they have. The only problem was that the stairs didn't match the elevator floors. When she reached the third door, she was only on the first floor; when she reached the sixth door, she was only on the second floor, and she needed to get to floor 7.

"Ugh, could this day get any worse! Now I have to use maths to find the floor." She stopped and reached far into her brain for her problem-solving techniques. "Right, what is the three times table song? It's not hard to count in 3s; it's just like swinging from the trees, 3,6,9 you'll be fine, 12,15,18 don't be unclean, 21... Yes, that's it! Floor 7 is the 21st door. Woo Hoo, maths rules! Oh wait, I hope no one heard that." Izzy looked around embarrassed, though she wasn't blushing, as cats don't blush. "Oh, that's right, I'm a cat. All they'll hear is a meow. Phew."

Izzy now swished her tail with excitement as she bounded up the stairs. A thought did creep into the back of her mind. She wished she could have told Lucia about her using maths to help. Lucia would always say Izzy was a maths genius, and even though Izzy didn't believe her, it made her smile inside every time she said it. It's nice to have your own personal cheerleader, and Lucia certainly made Izzy feel cheered for.

"Finally, door 21." Using her cat skills, Izzy pounced on the handle and rushed down the corridor looking for apartment 705. She bounced up and up like a spring until she flexed her paw and hit the doorbell. She heard a loud stomping towards the door. This was all becoming too easy. Maybe Lucia was right; being a cat does have its uses.

"Hello?" Fatima's mum looked in confusion around the corridor. As she was about to close the door, Izzy snuck in through the cat-sized gap and trotted the familiar route to Fatima's room, hearing the door slam shut behind her. VICTORY. She was in.

She jumped onto the bed and nuzzled into Fatima, relief painted on her cute cat face.

"ARGHHHH." Fatima sprung towards the ceiling and sent Izzy flying through the air, her fur bristling in shock.

Fatima's heart was pounding; a strange furry thing had just touched her. Then she surveyed the situation. "Wait, hang on. Cleo? Is that you?" Fatima took a step closer and then wiggled her nose in disgust. "Eww, you smell bad!" Fatima edged her hand carefully towards Cleo's collar to avoid the last of the camel poo and checked the name. "Yes, it's you. I can't believe it. Why are you here?" Fatima tickled Cleo (Izzy) under the chin.

"Fatima, it's me. You have to help. I'm in Cleo's body, and I think she's in mine."

But of course, Fatima only heard the dulcet tones of Cleo's Arabian Mau meows, not Izzy's pleas for a saviour. Fatima smiled sympathetically at who she thought was Cleo. Fatima tickled Izzy's chin, which did feel kind of nice for Izzy, even though she didn't want to admit it.

"I'll get my nanny to drop you home. I didn't even know cats could venture this far; it must have taken you hours to walk here. Hold that thought. I might ask her to give you a quick bath first."

The next thing Izzy knew was that she had been plunged into a cold-water lake covered in popping bubbles. A low growl could be heard from Izzy's cat throat. Bubbles gathered around Izzy's triangle ears, and her face was full of thunder. Everyone knows cats don't like water and especially don't like having a bath! They are perfectly capable of cleaning themselves much better than humans can.

So, after a quick bubble bath with Fatima's nanny – who was now covered in many tiny cat-sized scratches- Izzy was dropped back right where she had started – at home. Izzy's eyes prickled with frustration; cats couldn't cry, but inside Izzy's heart was a waterfall of tears spilling out. She had failed. Yet again, she couldn't do something and had let herself down. So, instead of crying, she let out a wail you can only hear from a cat in distress.

Finally, after a long and very loud wail, she let her mood lift. At least she was safe at home. She just had to reflect with Lucia and move forward.

Only problem was, Lucia was nowhere to be seen!

CHAPTER: 05

As soon as Izzy left the house to find Fatima, Lucia skipped up the stairs. She only had one place in mind. The spare bed! It was much bigger than her bed and always looked so comfortable. The pillows reminded her of fluffy marshmallows too delicious to eat. This was her chance. No one to tell her to tidy her room, no one to tell her to not make a mess with the covers. Even the thought of it was making Lucia feel dozy.

But she suddenly had a wave of guilt hit her like an earthquake. What if Izzy came back with some information and Lucia had done nothing? She would feel terrible.

Lucia reverted to the original plan; she knew she had to find one of her friends for some sort of help. How would she get to Liliana's, though? Liliana lived near the Marina, and Lucia knew it was far away because every time her parents dropped her there, she moaned how far away it was.

Excuse me, I don't moan every time we go to Liliana's, only when you put your rubbish music on in the front!

Lucia collected her girl gang like collecting mini brands. When she arrived at her school in Pre-KG, she knew this was where she was going to thrive. That level of confidence, even at the age of three, rippled through the room and hit Liliana first. She saw Lucia playing with the shapes so happily she wandered over and joined her game. Soon enough, their giggling attracted Felicity over, and curiosity overwhelmed Cora, who snuck over quietly (she was definitely the quietest of the group). From that day, more and more children gravitated towards their little gang of fun and laughter.

Lucia's mind started to drift, remembering the last time she played at Liliana's house. They had pretended they were entering a brand new dance competition that travelled around Dubai, teaching other children how to dance.

'One and Two and tuuuuurn,' Lucia directed the teddy bears learning the moves. 'Liliana, I think they have got it. They're ready for the big stage.'

'But are we ready, Lucia?' Liliana looked concerned (both girls forgetting this was a game).

'Liliana, we were born ready!'

All of Liliana's toys lined up and became a very respectful audience – Lucia thought they were the perfect audience as they didn't talk or go on their phones throughout the performance. She could hear the cheer and roar from the crowd as Liliana and Lucia ended in the splits, gasping for breath with smiles plastered on their faces.

'Focus, Lucia, focus!' Lucia shook her head back to reality. She had to try and think of a solution. It was too far to walk, even with her new cat energy. She can't drive because she, well, she's a cat. How could she contact Liliana? Mr Jackson would always tell Lucia to use her talk partner to share ideas. She then remembered when they were looking at different uses of paper, and her talk partner, Sultan, said toilet paper. She couldn't help but giggle in the middle of the lesson.

"How do you guys end up always making it about toilets, or poo or something silly," Mr Jackson sighed, but he did have a cheeky grin on his face as he swept his floppy blonde hair away from his twinkling eyes.

"Lucia, you've done it again!" Lucia shook her head until her whiskers quivered, but this seemed to have helped her with an idea.

"Talk partner... communicate... talk. When we were on distance learning, we used the computer to talk to our talk partner! That's it! I Zoom Liliana."

Lucia flew off the marshmallow bed and went in search of a laptop. The only problem was Lucia was distracted again, but this time, it was her bladder chatting to her instead of her talk partner. Lucia was bursting for a wee. Earlier, she had found it hilarious to drink from the cat fountain with her tongue and drank so much water. Now, she felt she was about to explode. Lucia rushed so fast to the toilet. She leapt, ready to finally feel the relief of the toilet. The only problem was she had forgotten she was a cat, a much smaller species, and she slammed straight INTO the toilet bowl.

Splash! Lucia plopped and flopped in the toilet and gurgled her way out of the toilet water. As she scrambled out the unhygienic swimming pool, her fur was slicked to her skin, drenched to her bones. Dripping all across the bathroom tiles, Lucia shook her fur and shivered with chill and anger. She looked like a drowned rat; well, she actually looked like a drowned cat, which is exactly what had nearly happened.

'Ugh, gross, toilet water is DIS-GUST-ING!' Lucia wished she didn't have an ultra-sensitive sense of smell as she was drenched with stale toilet water. Most humans don't smell the toilet water but definitely know they don't want to wash in it.

She remembered being a toddler and always being told, 'Don't touch that,' or 'yucky' when she tried to explore the toilet water. For a two-year-old, it looks like a fun toy. Now Lucia knew exactly why everyone always rushed to stop her. She dripped her way out of the bathroom, squelching and splashing as she stepped on each of her four paws towards the laptop.

52

Now, I am sure some of you have seen funny videos of cats trying to type on computers; it's hilarious! Well, this is exactly what Lucia looked like. Bashing and thrashing the keys, she tried, as carefully as she could, to type Z-O-O-M into the keyboard. Finally, after many attempts, she heard the ping of the zoom icon, and she used her nose to scroll down to the name Liliana.

The dull humming of the ring was mind-numbing for Lucia. Her patience was running out. When was Liliana going to answer the call??

"Hiiii, Lucia," Liliana's face popped up on the screen, and Lucia went into fast-forward mode.

"Liliana, you have to listen. Izzy and I have changed into cats. I know it's crazy, but it's true. I can show you my tail if you don't believe me."

But of course, yet again, all Liliana heard was the low-tone meow of Caesar vibrating through the screen.

"Caesar, what are you doing on the screen? How did you manage to ring me? You must be a clever cat, a noisy one too!" Liliana laughed to herself. "It's a shame Lucia isn't there; some of our friends are at the park near her house. What am I doing, talking to a cat?!" Liliana shook her head, laughing. "See ya later, Caesar." The screen flashed and then turned as black as the night. Liliana was gone.

As the screen reflected the mirror image of a cat in the blackness, Lucia thought about what Liliana had said; her other friends were at the park. If Lucia could just get to the park, they might be able to help. Luckily, she had seen Caesar take this route before. She let her mind daydream, this time to the memory of Caesar and Dad. One sunny day,

Mum, there was no need to include that. We live in Dubai. It is always sunny.

One normal day, Caesar was being his typical impish self and running up and down the garden wall, winding up the other cats on the other side. This was causing a huge commotion, as the other cats were growling and hissing at Caesar, making a huge noise. This led to Paul storming outside to sort out the situation, but Caesar was too clever for that. He jumped into the nearest tree, letting his ginger paws guide him with ease, then the next one and the next until suddenly it was like watching a monkey swing itself all the way to the park (when I say all the way, the park is at the end of the street). Now, Paul was not going to give up, so he ran out the front and raced down the street to meet Caesar at the park. However, Caesar had started running back to the house in his mischievous way, and Paul hadn't noticed until it was too late.

All of a sudden, Caesar was under Paul's feet, and just like a tree being chopped down, Paul tumbled to the floor with Caesar scampering back home with a cheeky flick of his tail. As Paul rubbed his bottom after landing straight on the pavement, Caesar was already curling up on the sofa, ready for an afternoon nap.

Lucia did giggle as she remembered her dad sprawled on the floor but then rapidly jumped into action. She raced to the garden wall and took a deep breath. The branches danced in the wind and suddenly looked more ominous than Lucia's memory. How was she going to focus and jump that far away? The floor looked even further away, and this now seemed like a very dangerous plan. Lucia took a deep breath and remembered what her teacher had said: 'Clear your mind and focus on what you want to achieve.' What she wanted to achieve was to land in the tree and not fall to her death at the bottom of the garden in Caesar's body. Lucia was more worried about hurting her precious cat's body with this perilous plan. She couldn't bear to know she was responsible for breaking his leg or tail with her incompetent jumping, but what choice did she have?

With that morbid thought, she launched herself into the air like an Emirates plane and leapt towards the upper branches. The cat instincts kicked in, and her claws protruded out of her paws, ready to catch the spindly branches. She clung on for her life and settled her paws onto the branch.

"I did it!" Lucia wanted to jump for joy but instantly knew this wouldn't be a good idea. She didn't want to test the theory of cats having nine lives.

A small part of her mind wanted Izzy to have seen her achievement.

Izzy was always Lucia's cheerleader; anytime Lucia got even a sticker for something, Izzy was there to celebrate with her. It's nice to have your own personal cheerleader, and Izzy certainly made Lucia feel cheered for.

Through the jungle-like trees, Lucia bounced with ease to the edge of the park, and her green eyes widened even further. She could see the gaggle of her girlies playing on the monkey bars, gripping from one bar to the next. Secretly, Lucia thought in her cat body, she'd be able to fly across the monkey bars much faster than them, but she was still impressed with her friends' achievements.

One of Lucia's friends looked up from the last bar of the monkey bars with a furrowed brow. 'Aww, look, isn't that Caesar? I wonder where Lucia is?" said Felicity. At this recognition, Lucia bounded down towards her friends. Felicity loved animals and straight away picked Lucia up in a huge, hard hug. Lucia felt all the air escape her body, and just before she thought she was about to be crushed, Felicity let her go. Before Lucia could catch her breath, the next friend scooped her up and held her like a baby.

'I've seen Caesar here before; this park is close to Lucia's house."

'IT IS ME, LUCIA!' but Lucia had already felt deflated even before she tried to speak. What was the use? Even her own mum didn't know it was her. How would her friends recognise the meows? Her already folded ears descended even further with disappointment. There is a certain look in a cat's eye when they are sad. It's impossible to describe, but if you've seen it, you will never forget it. This was the look that had currently washed over her face. Lucia had never felt this feeling before, and she never wanted to feel it again. It was loneliness. She felt like she was a tiny speck in the middle of a vast solar system where no one could hear her cries. The love she usually had in her heart was leaking out and being contaminated with this new and frightening feeling.

'Aww, look, maybe Caesar is hungry. That meowing is quite annoying. Let's go!' with that, the girls turned around to race to be the first ones on the swings and Lucia slunk home, knowing there was no dad to knock to the ground this time.

CHAPTER: 06

'Lucia, Lucia!' Izzy bounded from one room to the next, panting as she went. The panic was rising up in her again like a bubbling volcano. 'Lucia, where are you?' Izzy could smell the dripping of musty toilet water around the house. What had happened since she had been away?

'LLLLUUUCCCIII-'

'Hi,' Lucia said, popping her orange head around the corner of the door.

Is no one worried at this point that the door has been left open the entire time?! *It's Dubai. It would be more of a surprise if the door was closed.* **I suppose it is pretty safe here, but still, not a good advert for responsible parenting.**

Izzy jumped half a metre backwards, forgetting her own cat agility. 'Oh Lucia, I was so worried, where have you been?'

'I've been at the park looking for help. Hang on, why do you smell of, hmm, what is that smell? It's a hint of bubbles, a smell of grass, a trace of cactus and a huge whiff of poo! Where have you been?' Lucia took a step back from Izzy, who had obviously not had all of the camel poo washed off properly. It might have something to do with all the scratching and moaning she did when getting her 'relaxing' bath.

'I'll explain later. Did you get any help at the park?'

'No, just a lot of squeezing, you?'

'Nope, just a lot of bottoms in my face.' Lucia looked confused, 'I will explain later, I promise. So, what do we do now?'

'I don't know, you're the eldest, what do you think?'

'Right, well, I think we need to figure out what we know to find out what we need to know. So...' The girls shared everything they had learned so far, from the minute they were sent to their rooms to this very moment on the sofa (Lucia managed to get them both curled up back on the sofa again).

'I remember it raining,' said Lucia.

'Then there was a flash of light,' replied Izzy.

'Then all I remember is waking up in the morning.'

'So, the flash of light is our last memory of being in our own bodies. I know Cleo was asleep next to me, and Caesar must have been asleep next to you.'

'Hmm,' Lucia had drifted off and was licking her paws clean from the adventures of the day so far.

'Focus Lucia! The flash of light, the cats being next to us, it's all linked!'

'But right now, the cats are wherever Mum and Dad are, with our bodies. Soooo, we aren't next to them just now. What's your next bright idea?'

The girls were stumped. They had no idea where their family was this weekend. They were always going around Dubai during their weekends; sometimes, it felt like they were on a guided tourist tour, but they secretly loved it once they got there. They had an inkling their parents had told them - more than once - but there was a slight chance they weren't listening at the time.

You definitely didn't tell us. **Yes, we never knew. You never tell us anything!**

After Lucia had finished licking her paws and, of course, had another huge stretch, she started to come up with ideas, even if they were the wrong ones.

'I'm sure they mentioned something about going to the waterpark?' Lucia suggested.

'No, Lucia. YOU suggested going to the waterpark, it was a firm no from Mum and Dad. Mum has just had her hair dyed and didn't want to get it wet, remember?'

'They definitely said something about the water park,' Lucia grumbled.

'No, it was something about the aquarium,' Izzy suggested, though she hadn't even convinced herself.

'No WAY. Dad hates the busy queues. There's no way he'd want to go there on the weekend!"

'Did."
'Didn't."
'Did,"
'Didn't."

SSSTTTOPPPPPP!

The girls froze with confusion. Everyone was out of the house. Where had this distant voice come from? Lucia began to tremble as Izzy crept slowly towards the stairs.

EEEENNNOUGGHHH.

There it was again. The mysterious voice quietly rumbled through the house. Lucia's teeth were now chattering, and she had slunk behind Izzy.

'It's coming from upstairs," Lucia whispered as quietly as a mouse. Both girls switched on their ninja cat stealth mode and silently crept up the stairs. With each step, Lucia heard her heartbeat getting louder and louder. Who was in their house? Were they in danger? Her brain was fluttering with the flames of fear. She wanted her and her sister to stay safe. Izzy led the way, trying to be the heroic one, but in her stomach, she could feel it knotting with trepidation. She must keep her sister safe, but how?

In Izzy's room, they could hear a voice grumbling and moaning from behind the door. The girls froze again. Their feet felt like they had been iced to the floor. This was a voice they had never heard before. There was a stranger in their house. An UNINVITED stranger. Why was this person in Izzy's room?

'Should we sneak in?' whispered Izzy, turning around and nearly bumping into Lucia as she was so close behind her. She was nearly next to her bum.

'No way! I'm not going in there,' hissed Lucia.

'Well, what's your bright idea?'

"THIS IS EXACTLY WHAT I WAS TALKING ABOUT!"

The strange, low voice suddenly echoed from inside the room, and the girls had a realisation.

It was Bagel.

CHAPTER: 07

You do know you didn't tell them about Bagel, right? So, as he's mine, I feel I should take over for a second. Bagel is my hamster, and he lives in my room. I know what you're thinking: Bagel is a weird name for a hamster. Well, in lockdown, we had to look after the class hamster, and his name was Toast. Mum says Toast saved her sanity during lockdown because he kept us busy. I mean, this was sort of true. We loved making different obstacle courses for him and clearing out his cage, which took ages. But then we got Cleo, and Toast had to go to another family. *Don't tell them what happened there. It's bad.* Well, now I have to tell them. There was a kids party, and there were loads of balloons. Hamsters can suffer from heart attacks if they're scared, and all the balloons frightened Toast. Luckily, he survived the party and ran on his wheel happily. Some time later, when everyone had gone home, someone sneezed, and it was such a loud sneeze he had a heart attack. *Let's get back to Bagel.* Yes, so we thought when I got my hamster, we should stick to the bakery theme in honour of Toast, so he was named Bagel. I usually have to keep my door closed, as Caesar had knocked the cage over a few times. One night, Caesar knocked the cage over, and Mum and Dad had to run around my room chasing Bagel and Caesar like a Tom and Jerry cartoon. I just slept soundly, with no idea what was going on.

'Was that who I thought it was?' Lucia looked at Izzy, then back to Bagel and back to Izzy again.

"Could this day get any weirder?!" Both Izzy and Lucia swished their tails while they stared in disbelief at Bagel's cage. Inside was the small Dwarf Hamster munching on a piece of carrot with a cantankerous look on his mink-coloured face.

"Yes, it is; who do you think it is? Oh, and by the way, I'm sick of you two." Bagel twitched his nose and glared at Izzy and Lucia angrily. His tiny teeny whiskers vibrated on his face with a little wiggle.

"I don't know why, but there is something about him that is making him look like a McDonald's Happy Meal." Lucia licked her lips, and Izzy had saliva running down her furry chin.

"Don't you two even think about it." Bagel could see the hunger in their eyes. "Okay, I can see you two are confused. Cleo, Caesar and I have come to an agreement ever since Caesar tried to eat me for the third time. It was becoming highly inconvenient, to say the least. We decided that I wouldn't bite them if they didn't break my cage." The girls still just stared vacantly at the tiny, little hamster speaking to them, yes, that's right, speaking to THEM, and they were UNDERSTANDING. If cats could pinch themselves, they would.

"So let me get this straight. Can you speak to Cleo and Caesar?"

"Yes, of course, it's better than listening to you two argue. I've heard the whole story, so no need to recap it for me. I've heard you two tell a story before, and it takes you FOREVER. Plus, they're always so boring, all about your teachers or some girl called Fatima and Liliana." Bagel yawned loudly then continued. "Anyway, I knew this morning you had switched bodies. Caesar normally comes in and sniffs my cage before you wake up," he paused, pointing his minuscule little paw at Izzy while she continued to look shocked- though she does remember constantly waking up to Caesar in her room looking pleased with himself.

"Well, if you know so much, you probably also know," Izzy rolled her eyes with exacerbation, 'where did Mum and Dad go?

'Of course I know that. I hear everything in this house.' Bagel squeaked, his small black eyes glinting with excitement. He had a plan brewing. 'They did tell you both plenty of times but neither of you were listening. Hmm what will you do for me if I tell you?' 'Anything!' Lucia pounced towards him, her face peering closely into the cage. Usually, this would put Bagel on edge having Caesar that close to his cage, but obviously, it wasn't 'Caesar' today.

'I want that nice cereal you both eat on the weekends; you always smell of it when you come upstairs and it seems so delici-'

'Deal.' Lucia interrupted and started to turn and leave the room. 'Hang on.' Izzy interrupted. There was a lot of interrupting going on at this point of the day. 'Lucia, did you forget that we have cat bodies? We can't just pick it up out of the cupboard.'

Lucia paused, 'Let's just use our paws.' Lucia suggested.

'Don't be silly, we can't do that.'

'But we need to try.'

'What's the point, it's impossible.'

'This is exactly what got you two in this mess in the first place. You're always arguing and not helping each other. Work it out, then I'll help you.' Bagel turned around and started nuzzling into his sawdust, ready for a nap. I mean, he had the right idea; he knew these two working together might take a while.

Both girls raced down the stairs and stared patiently at the cupboard door, waiting for one of them to come up with an amazing idea.

"Soooo…."

"Soooo."

"I think Bagel was right," Izzy edged towards Lucia, "we need to stop arguing so much."

"I agree," Lucia tiptoed towards Izzy, "I know we can't hug right now, but should we have a little snuggle?" They rubbed up against each other. I know this seems strange for two sisters, but they were cats, and it was as close to a hug as they could manage. If you've ever seen cats get along, you will recognise this. Once they had had their cute little moment, they started to formulate a plan. Out of the blue, Lucia sprinted towards the cupboard, slamming her head into the closed door.

"WHAT ARE YOU DOING?" Izzy rushed over to Lucia, who was staggering backwards.

"It worked… didn't it?" The girls glanced behind them, and it seemed Lucia's (well, Caesar's, really) head was the perfect equipment for opening the cupboard door.

"Nice work, Lucia," Lucia grinned, well as much as a cat could smile. She couldn't believe she had made her sister proud. Her whole body felt like it had grown 10 cm taller.

Now, it was all nose power. The girls didn't have hands, so they used the next best thing: their noses. They managed to manoeuvre the cereal box to the bottom of the stairs. Then, with each step, it took an almighty flip to launch it onto the next one. If anyone had watched this from the window and videoed it, I'm sure it would have had a million likes on YouTube.

It was crazy to see, but they managed it, and with a huge puff of breath, they put the box beside Bagel's cage. Bagel slowly glanced in their direction, then curled up again, unimpressed.

"Only one more thing, girls," Bagel yawned loudly, "I can't open it." Both girls grinned at each other and winked.

"Are you ready? After three, two, one... GO!" They both sprung into the air and landed on the cereal box, spraying bits of bran flakes and sugared corn across the room that rained on top of Bagel through the grates of his cage.

"Mmm thank-mmm- you mm- they-mm w-mm-ent to the desert for a barbecue."

As Bagel lay in his new cage of dreams, basting in the cereal flakes, the girls sighed.

'So, somewhere nice and easy to find them?!'

CHAPTER: 0.2

I think it's important to know how your day is going, Mum. **Yes, it can't have been easy having Cleo and Caesar running around the desert like, like, well, like cats!** *Let's have a small interlude from us and see what's happening with the rest of the family.* **Interlude!? Loving the word, Lucia! Thanks.**

As Paul entered the quiet morning road, he let out a sigh of relief whilst zooming down the silent desert road. Luckily for the family, no one else was up at the same time as them. Izzy and Lucia's mum loves an early start to make the most of the day.

Early start, try the middle of the night!

"That was a weird start to the day. Those cats haven't been spooked by a storm before." Paul looked in his rearview mirror at the two 'girls' sitting in the back, hands squashed onto the windows, looking out intently at the speeding view. "And Izzy and Lucia are not their 'usual' selves either. I mean, we have been driving for nearly half an hour, and they haven't argued at all."

The girl's mum also took a concerned look behind her. Cleo and Caesar, in the girls' bodies, were now sniffing each other and trying to get out of their seatbelts with little success. "I know, I'm enjoying the peace, but there's something I can't quite put my finger on with those two. It's like it isn't them." She left that thought lingering in the car as they sped towards the desert.

As they had left so early in the morning...

Alright, we get it, early starts are your thing.

...the Collins family arrived at the desert with the whole day to enjoy hanging out in the sand. The moment the car doors opened, Cleo and Caesar jumped out on their two human feet and fell smack straight into the sand.

"Have you two never walked before? You have two feet for a reason." Paul tutted at the girls as they struggled to stand up. It was like watching a baby giraffe taking its first steps, only they had two human legs. Cleo and Caesar finally managed to get up, and both of them froze. Then sprang into action. A small insect had caught their attention, and both of them went bounding after it, catapulting into another pile of sand. Now, the next bit gets even weirder. Once they fell into the sand, they used their human tongues to start licking their arms, legs and-_and-_ (I don't know if I can say this bit...)

Say it!

...and their bums! Now, of course, they had clothes on because they were humans at the moment, but they were trying their hardest to slither into a position of licking their bums clean from all the sand. They looked like they were tying themselves in an impossible knot while letting their tongues hang out, ready for the perfect clean. Both Paul and their mum stared in disbelief at them. They sprang into action and quickly scurried over and rushed them back to their things, with their cheeks getting redder and redder (and not from the Sun).

'What has got into these two!?' Paul sighed as he pulled Caesar (in Lucia's body) back in the direction of where they had set up camp. The girls' mum followed with Izzy, and they both plonked the girls on their blankets.

In an instant, both girls yawned, stretched and started walking around and around in a circle. Finally, they sat down and curled into what looked like a very comfortable nap.

Both parents stared in astonishment. 'It's going to be a long day!'

CHAPTER: 08

Even though Bagel was a grumpy and greedy hamster, something he had said had flicked a switch in both of their minds. They had to work together to solve this crisis, so in unison, they bounded out of the house (leaving the door open again) and raced down to the end of the street. The only way to get to the desert that fast was to catch the Metro. The girls had a special memory of the Metro, so they were excited to hop on.

The Metro was the train line system in Dubai that ran alongside Sheikh Zayed Road but was cleaner, quicker and traffic-free. When the Collins family first moved to Dubai, they took the daunting journey on the Metro from the airport to their first apartment. The girls stared in wonder outside the windows at the mesmerising skyline, and they instantly fell in love with the city. Now, as cats, they had to face this journey again, but they were not going to get the luxury of sitting in Gold class gawking out in peace and quiet. They had never seen cats on the Metro, and they had a funny feeling they might not be welcome.

The Metro station is like a mini train station, just a lot cleaner! It has everything you would expect: ticket machines, barriers, escalators. Only problem was Izzy and Lucia were staring at it from a cat's perspective, which is A LOT lower than a human. As they gazed up at the automatic doors, they took a deep breath and waited for the crowds to walk through and set off the sensor. Like unlocking a vault, the doors swiped open, and Izzy and Lucia leapt in, battling with the throngs of feet stomping like elephants.

(Disclaimer: I'm not calling these people elephants. That would be very rude. I'm using a simile to help you understand how Izzy and Lucia felt taking on the obstacle course of the entrance).

What they hadn't accounted for were the 'other' guests at the entrance! A large gang of four stray cats lounged under one of the benches, smelling their way along the edges of the windows, scouring for food. There was a clear leader of the pack who would have even made Izzy and Lucia feel cautious in their human bodies. His jagged teeth looked like they could rip through an enemy's flesh with ease, each one laced with a thick layer of grime from eating off the streets. Patches of fur were missing from his back, inevitably from a multitude of battles in the dusty streets of Jumeriah. Unlike Caesar's green glowing eyes or Cleo's amber crescent eyes, this cat's eyes shone black with menace, telling stories of fights in the darkness.

The other cats weren't much nicer. One had a missing ear that looked like it had been chewed by a dog, one had a limp in its back leg, and one was covered in dust and mud from days of not washing and hiding under cars. Together, they seemed like a group of pirate cats, just without the parrots and peg legs.

The girls turned their cat noses up at the gang in disgust. The smell wafted over to them and got trapped in their noses, making them want to gag. Without warning, the head of the gang turned his ugly head towards the girls and let a menacing grin grow on his face. He boldly strode over to the girls, with the gang following like the bad smell they were. Izzy and Lucia cowered into a corner, teeth chattering and paws shaking.

'Who are you two?' His spit landed on Izzy's face, dripping down her jaw.

'We are Iz-,' Izzy poked Lucia in the side to stop her from getting it wrong,

'Cleo and Caesar, we just need to get to the desert,'

'Ooooh,' the whole gang began to cackle at the girls, saliva spitting everywhere like a shower. The sound of stray cats laughing is a very weird one. It is like a mix of a dog whimpering and a chicken clucking. Cats are usually very serious and hardly ever laugh, so this is why hardly anyone knows what this sounds like. Scientists have done experiments and different studies to try to make cats laugh, but it never works; they are far too serious.

'You must be new around here. I am Fluffy,' the lead cat introduced himself, and Lucia stifled a snigger. 'This is Baz, Maz and Laz.' He pointed round to the rest of the gang. The one covered in dust gave Izzy a strange look, which put Izzy on edge. He was beginning to edge closer and closer to her.

'Tell 'em fluffy, tell 'em.' One of Baz, Maz or Laz said; the girls didn't know which one.

"You can't be here, this is our patch." Fluffy flexed his muscles in his legs and revealed his gnarly teeth. The smell of rotten fish hit the air.

The one covered in dust (they thought it was Laz) was still staring at Izzy with the weirdest look on his face. "I like your orange spots," Laz said to Izzy, his tongue beginning to hang out of his mouth. "You have eyes."

"Okaaay?!" Izzy answered wearily, then snapped back to Fluffy. "Look, Fluffy, we only need to get on the Metro, we won't be here very long."

Another strange dog/chicken laugh rang through the entrance to the Metro. All the people jumping on and off the Metro were taking no notice of the 'conversation' that was happening between the newly acquainted cats. If anyone had stopped to look at what was going on, two family cats being cornered by a group of mangy strays, they may have stepped in, but everyone was too busy with their own day to worry about a gang of cats.

"Sorry, Cleany, Clee-oo? Whatever your name was, it doesn't work like that. You and your friend, what was it Geezer? Sneezer? Better get lost quick. You don't want to know how I got this scar." Fluffy turned around to show the whole group a huge spiky scar running from the top of his back to his tail...

Top of his back to his tail, Mum, isn't that just his bum? Don't be so lame, you can say it, you know.

A huge, spiky scar running across his entire bottom.

"Aww boss, can't we keep that one," Laz pointed (well waved his paw) at Izzy, "I think I have fallen in love with her."

"WHAT?!" There was a unison of confusion from every single cat - even Laz joined in just so he wasn't left out. He wasn't the brightest of cats.

'Excuse me?' Izzy couldn't hide the disgust in her voice. 'I am only 9 years old!'

'You're nine? You look much younger than that. How do you keep your fur so smooth? Please, boss, please, can't we keep her?'

Izzy realised that Laz had fallen in love with CLEO. Now she knew cats didn't wait around to fall in love, and she also knew that Cleo was a stunning and beautiful cat. I mean, she was her pet, she was amazing. But she also knew Cleo was much better than this filthy, idiotic thing.

Lucia nudged Izzy. This whole situation was getting too weird for her liking, and she knew they had to get to the desert fast before her parents went somewhere else.

'What do we do?' Lucia hissed under her breath, in that way where you don't want anyone to see your mouth moving.

'I have a plan, do you trust me?' Lucia winked an acknowledgement at Izzy.

'Laz...?' Izzy moved closer to Laz, plan in action.

'Yes, yes Cleo, anything, what is it?'

'What is that weird thing over there?'

'What weird thi-'

"RUN!" Izzy and Lucia pounded over the gang of cats and galloped across the entrance. They swerved through the crowds, like on a Super Sonic Game trying to catch the golden rings. Close behind them, Fluffy and his gang sprinted to keep up, Fluffy bashing Laz any time he came close with a furious punch.

Left turn. Fluffy got closer.

Right turn. He was nearly at their tails.

Straight ahead. Izzy could smell his fishy breath behind her, but she was determined to keep going. They reached the escalator, and Izzy and Lucia knew the trick. Humans stand on the right and walk on the left. It is just one of those rules no one teaches you, but every human knows it. This gave them that well-needed advantage. They raced up the left side while Fluffy and his gang got stuck behind a family of four, trying to force their pram onto the escalator. Even though there are lifts, you will always find one family that wants to break the rules and try to squeeze the pram on the escalator. The dad was battling with the lever to fold up the complicated pram, and the mum was battling with two children screaming into her tired ears.

This was just the luck Izzy and Lucia needed. They bounded to the top and saw the Metro doors open. Izzy got her paw caught in the escalator and let out a blood-curdling screech. Nevertheless, she knew she had to carry on. As quick as a flash, they soared in the air through the automatic doors as they swished closed. On the other side of the clean glass, four cat faces crashed into the glass, leaving an imprint of fur and unhappy faces, and the girls sped away on the highspeed Metro.

CHAPTER: 09

Looking out the pristine windows, the girls intently watched the exquisite city they had grown to love whoosh past. As they passed each landmark and it disappeared into the distance, they knew the desert was getting forever closer. Each time they heard the security guard walk down the aisles, they dipped under the cushioned seats to hide away from being caught. They didn't want to get this far and be thrown off the Metro at a random stop. They found themselves cuddling into each other to stay safe. Gradually, each one began to purr at the serenity of taking a moment to pause on this crazy day.

"You know, even though this day has been horrendous, difficult, and downright weird. It has been good to spend some time with you, Izzy."

"I know what you mean. I've been so busy lately worrying about stuff I feel like we haven't done any of the things we used to. Remember when we would go out on the scooters all the way to the beach? And remember when the security guard was trying to chase after us because we weren't allowed scooters on the beach." Izzy drifted into the memory.

"Yes, Mum was so embarrassed she pretended to talk to that old man so the security guard didn't notice her. But hang on, what have you been so worried about?"

"You know, just school stuff."

"I don't know," sighed Lucia, curling up even closer to Izzy, "you're always so mean to me at school."

"I just... well, I've been finding maths tricky for ages. I think I'm worried you're going to be better at maths than me, and I'm two years older than you. What happens if I get kicked out of school?"

Izzy hung her furry little head, seeming as small as a mouse sheltering under the seat.

"Izzy, are you mad? Look at all the ways you have problem-solved today. So what, you don't know, 7x7? Isn't that what calculators are for?"

Izzy chuckled at her sister, "I'm sorry I was mean, but in fairness, you do wind me up."

"I know, everyone always thinks I'm the 'funny one' so sometimes I wind you up to make people laugh. I'm sorry. I'm not like you, I don't ask all the questions and have interesting conversations. If I am not funny, then what will people like about me?"

"Lucia," Izzy tucked her paw onto Lucia's with a small wince, it was still wounded from the escalator, "you are funny, but when you are trying not to be. You are the most optimistic person I know. The glass isn't half full, it's brimming over the edges, it's so full."

Lucia's whiskers twitched as she smiled at her sister. They both jumped back up onto the seats to enjoy the journey. Now they were away from Downtown, the Metro was much quieter, and they could continue to stare out the window at the sand dunes that rushed past their eyes, looking like they were dancing in the scorching sky.

'Oh, look over there,' Lucia nudged Izzy to the right of the window, 'a caravan of camels.' Out of the window, in the distance, there were camels strolling through the dunes aimlessly.

'Please, don't talk to me about camels!' Izzy went on to explain what had happened on the way to Fatima's house earlier that day, and the girls howled with laughter as their city disappeared behind them. Under all the laughing and the talking, there was a sinking feeling in both of the girls' hearts. What were they going to do when they finally found their parents... and their bodies!

Finally, after what felt like an eternity, they heard the familiar sound.

Almahatat altaaliat hi Bar Dubay. المحطة التالية هي بر دبي

Now, the girls don't speak Arabic...

Umm, excuse me, I do Arabic at school, and I can say lots of things. *Me too, I can say I love my mum and my dad in Arabic, that's useful.*

Anyway, because they had been on the Metro so many times, they knew the Arabic words to listen out for. Next stop, Bur Dubai.

'Now you know what that means. One more stop on this line, and then it's straight on the new line to the desert.' Izzy impatiently looked out the window. In their excitement, they didn't notice the looked out the window. In their excitement, they didn't notice the security guard storming towards them, his eyebrows fixed in a grimacing frown. He knew that cats weren't allowed on the Metro. How had these two stragglers got on here?

'Right, you two,' he grabbed both Izzy and Lucia by the scruffs of the neck, 'this is your last stop; no animals on the Metro!' As the automatic door slid open, he threw the cats onto the grimy grey platform. Only problem was, this wasn't their stop!

CHAPTER: 10

For anyone who has not been to Dubai, Bur Dubai is the older end of Dubai, but it is full of rich history. The girls usually love to explore the hidden alleys with their secrets, but today was a different story. As they reluctantly descended the escalator, Lucia nearly got her tail caught, but luckily, her cat instincts swished it away just in time; they stepped out onto the bustling street. Their heightened cat senses were bombarded with a symphony of colours. It was like a canvas painting of history. People on bikes and scooters rushed past, ready to head to the souks. The call to prayer rang through the streets, and men sauntered closer to the Mosque, which was by the rippling canal. The canal was integral to Dubai's trade and development. Abras bobbed up and down the mouth of the canal, ready to cross from one side to the other on their daily journey, reflecting in the crystal waters.

Mum loves going to the Creek and exploring old Dubai, can you tell? **I mean, we do, too, but I think Mum really wants you to picture it so you can imagine it for yourselves.**

As they strolled down the alleyways, the girls suddenly realised they were now on the wrong side of the canal. Problem number one.

They also knew that in this part of town, there was only one way across.

This was: Problem number two.

As the girls trotted through the souks (this is the Arabic word for market), they could see the mountains of spices piled up in front of each shop. The smell of saffron, cardamon, and cinnamon floated through the streets as they made their way to the water's edge.

'Do you think we could just grab a small bit of food while we are here?' asked Lucia, as her nose picked up on the smells of Shawarma from the markets.

'No, we will surely be caught, and we have no time to waste. This is a massive detour for us.' But Izzy's nose had also caught the smell of the succulent chicken marinading in aromatic spices. They continued their path through the bustling streets and avoided the crowds of feet stamping through the town. Past the Gold Souk, where the shops twinkled, the sun kissed the array of jewelry being displayed.

'Maybe we could stop here for a bit an-'

'No way, Izzy.' Lucia nudged her with her nose, 'we would definitely get caught here! And besides, what would you do with gold jewelry while you are a cat? Get a gold-encrusted collar!?' Lucia giggled to herself as they made their way towards the salty smell of the canal.

"What are we going to do?" asked Izzy. This was problem number two. The vast canal splashed towards their swishing tails that were instinctively avoiding the water. It was a HUGE problem that neither of them wanted to deal with but both girls knew there was only one thing to do as they watched the Abras sail across the canal gracefully, filled with people from all around the world.

"After three, one... two... THREEEE, GO!" Both girls used all their might to launch themselves towards the Abra that had set sail across the canal. With a bump, Lucia gave herself a quick shake and checked her body. Shocked, but all fine. Suddenly, she darted her eyes around, she couldn't see Izzy anywhere.

"IZZZZZZYYYYYY!"

Let's rewind ten seconds...

"After three, one... two... THREEEE, GO!" as Izzy launched into the air, her injured paw gave way, and her jump failed, leaving her crashing towards the salty water below.

"Izzy? Izzy?" screamed Lucia, "Where are you?"

"Lu-mmm," Izzy went under the water and reappeared again, coughing and spluttering, "Lucia, I'm here-mmm!" Down under, she went again. Cats notoriously hate water and can't swim. Right now, Izzy was behind the bobbing Abra, barely staying above the water.

"Izzy!" The fear in Lucia's voice was clear to anyone who could speak cat. Her sister was in danger, and she didn't know what to do. She usually had a team of friends to help her with any problem or her sister to support her. But now she was left on her own on the boat with her sister drowning in the crystal water below.

"Think Lucia, think!" her eyes moved at lightning speed around the Abra, looking for inspiration. She suddenly caught a glimpse of the lifebuoy next to the edge of the wooden Abra. With all her strength, she nudged the buoy with her nose. Little by little, it began to wobble off its holder.

In the lapping water, Izzy was rapidly losing energy. Each time she went underwater, she spluttered the salty liquid out with a rasping cough. How long could she keep this up?

Lucia kept pushing and pushing the lifebuoy towards the edge of the Abra. Luckily, people in Dubai are used to cats wandering around, so they didn't give Lucia any attention at all.

SPLASH!

Finally, the buoy smacked into the water. All Izzy had to do was swim to it, but she was nearly at her exhaustion limit.

Lucia looked into the water at her own reflection. She knew what to do. With that, she plunged into the water and swam (well, a sort of doggy paddle - it should be called catty paddle really) towards Izzy. With her teeth, she grabbed Izzy's tail and pulled her towards the buoy. Lucia used all her strength to heave Izzy to the safety of the buoy. It felt like time had stood still as Lucia hooked Izzy onto the buoy and grabbed on herself, panting violently. They both hung onto the neon orange doughnut-shaped buoy, gasping for breath. But at least they were safe, for now!

By the time they reached the other side of the creek, the girls had quite enjoyed their water ride. Once they got the hang of holding on with their paws, they balanced carefully and enjoyed the free water ride. They clambered onto the side of the port and shook off the warm, salty water. As it was Dubai, they dried off in minutes and continued their journey through the secret streets.

'Lucia, that was amazing. You were so brave,' Izzy curled her tail around Lucia in appreciation.

'I couldn't leave my sister behind. You're part of me.' As the girls scurried around the tall buildings, whispering tales of traditions, they pondered what was their next move.
'So the Metro is out, we can't drive or get a taxi. We can't walk to the desert. So how are we going to get there?' Lucia looked to her sister for guidance.

'How else do we get around in Dubai?' Izzy wondered.

'We always go in Dad's car... or by bike to the beach, I guess. We can only do that when the bike wheels are pumped up. Remember when Dad tried to pump the air up at the petrol station, and he got so annoyed and nearly threw the bikes down the stree-'

'Hang on, what did you say?'

'About Dad getting annoyed at the petrol station, he kept saying words under his breath that I think he wasn't supposed to sa-'

'No, you said bikes! What's like a bike but quicker?'

Lucia thought for a moment, 'I think I know this joke...'

'Lucia, it's not a joke. Scooters! The town is full of them. They're faster, MUCH faster than bikes, and they go everywhere.'

"But how do we get one to go to the desert? We could be driving around town for hours."

"Wait here." Izzy skipped over to a nearby café with people sipping Karak and coffee. It was a traditional café with Arabic patterns painted on the outside of the crumbling bricks. Inside, there were intricate blue tiles from floor to ceiling covering the entire café. This cooled the café down to suit the Dubai summer weather. The tables were small, black outdoor tables with legs that curled round and round to create spiral shapes at the bottom. As this was an old café, some of the tables wobbled on their rusting legs. Some people had balanced cardboard underneath the table legs to try and stop their coffee spilling everywhere. Each table had miniature clay pots teetering on the edges, stuffed with napkins for the inevitable spills.

"There!" She dashed to what looked like an empty table and jumped onto it. But the table wasn't empty. It had two phones and a set of car keys left on the side, clinking as Izzy disrupted the table.

In Dubai, people leave their most valuable things to reserve their table. Mad but true. Mum does it all the time when she goes up to order our food.

She used her nose to navigate through the phone to Noon Food.

"What are you doing?" Lucia raced over to investigate what her sister was doing, wondering if the seawater had gone to her head.

"If I order from this restaurant to the desert, one of these drivers will hop on his scooter to the exact location I request. As soon as we see it move, we hop on and join the ride." Izzy grinned. "2 coffees and a Fattoush salad, that should do it."

"Hang on, Izzy, when we get there, who is going to pay for the coffees? This isn't fair." Lucia's moral compass went into overdrive. She could not stand for anyone to be cheated.

"I know I get it, but what choice do we have? We can owe them back when we get out of this mess." Izzy's eyes glanced over an extra option. "Shall I order an extra dessert?"

Lucia thought for a little while, making an internal promise to right the wrongs of today. Then, her stomach took over.

"Always." Lucia laughed.

It didn't take long for one of the delivery drivers in their yellow outfits to rush inside the café and return back with a brown paper bag in his hand. As he placed the food into the back of his bike, the girls jumped into action.

"This is not going to be a comfortable ride!" Izzy grimaced.

The girls squeezed their tiny cat-sized bottoms onto the back of the bike and used their curled claws to dig into the fabric of the seat to hold on for dear life. This driver knew he had to get the food to the desert in record time, so he swerved and dashed through the traffic with expert precision.

'I think I'm going to be siiiiiick!' Izzy wailed while the driver took a sharp turn to the right.

'I knooooow!' Lucia screeched as her back leg flew off the seat, and she wobbled dramatically.

'Lucia!' Izzy used her one free paw to grab Lucia back into safety and clung onto her tightly.

Green, orange, red, green, orange, red. The traffic lights were constantly changing like a light show. As the driver saw a long stretch of straight road, he took the opportunity to rev his engine and speed up. As they zoomed forward, the cats' mouths vibrated and wobbled due to the speed.

Finally, the driver saw the Al Qudra exit, deviated sharply and pulled on the brakes. The driver looked confused. There was no one waiting for an order of extra desserts, only two cats wobbling around the empty street. After a few phone calls and an angry face, the driver got back on his scooter and sped off into the distance.

"Phew. I'm glad that's over." The girls staggered around like their parents after brunch and tried to get their feet back to normal.

"Well, that was easy…NOT?!" Both girls collapsed laughing, elated to be one step closer to their family.

CHAPTER: II

Huffing and puffing, they stepped forward and felt the oven heat hit their bodies. They took a moment just to take in the majestic view in front of them. For miles and miles, sand dunes stretched as far as the horizon. Sand tickled their noses, and it brushed past them in the wind. Scatterings of bushes speckled the desert, and the odd camel wandered by. The calmness of the atmosphere instantly left the girls feeling at ease. They began to hear the familiar sounds of chatting and laughing from the many people in Dubai who drive out to the desert to enjoy the countryside. Now, I know it might sound strange; sand, countryside? But it really is amazing. It feels like you have stepped onto Planet Mars. There aren't rows of lush trees or meadows of wildflowers like in other countries, but the sky is clear, and the sand is warm on your feet.

Only problem is, have you ever seen a cat trying to walk on sand? It was not a skill the girls were used to. They were used to wearing their trainers and hiking through the sand with a little pull from their Dad. He would use his two hands to grab each girl and drag them as quickly as he could. It was a great game and made it much easier to travel through the sand. Unfortunately, cats have small paws that aren't as big as children's feet. Science tells us there are more vibrations in the sand when you walk on it, and sand acts similar to water as the grains of sand are miniscule...

Boring, come on, it's not school now. Just say that the cats kept sinking into the sand.

Izzy and Lucia, being in the bodies of Cleo and Caesar, kept sinking into the sand. It was like watching someone wade through a pool of baked beans. Not sure why that image came into my head, but I hope it helps you imagine the predicament they were in. With each step they took, the harder it was to get across the sand. One step. Stuck. Another step. Stuck. And it didn't help, each time Lucia toppled over, Izzy started giggling.

Lucia scowled at Izzy, "Sorry, I can't help it, you have to admit it is funny, it's so fu-" At that, Izzy tried to take a step forward on her front paw, and she fell face first, spitting and spluttering out grains of sand.

"You're right," Lucia cackled, "it is a bit funny." This comical journey continued for what felt like a year (it was about ten minutes) until they heard a familiar voice.

"What are those two doing now? They've been more than weird all day."

Izzy and Lucia shook the sand out of their eyes and spun around. To the right, where everyone had a perfect view of the sunset, they could see their dad, Paul, pulling a funny facial expression. Then they realised why. Their bodies (Cleo and Caesar's brains) were wandering around, trying to sniff each other's bottoms and then batting each other away with their hands.

"Oh, how embarrassing. Look at what those two are doing with our bodies!"

"I hope there's no one here we know," replied Lucia.

"No wonder Dad looks so confused, they must have had a crazy day today with those two cats, humans, oh I don't know what to call them now!" Izzy wondered for a moment if her parents had enjoyed their day with Cleo and Caesar more than being with them and their arguing. She let her mind wander to the consequences of arguing with Lucia and if they had trapped themselves in cats' bodies for good. Then she remembered they couldn't give up, they were too close and had worked too hard.

Now, their end goal was in sight; they used all their determination to get closer to their families and hopefully back to normality, but Izzy paused just before voyaging over the final sand dune.

"What is it?" Lucia paused and waited for Izzy to catch up, but she didn't. That nagging thought had crept back into her mind like one of those annoying mosquitos at night you can hear but never find.

"This morning, Dad just threw you out of the car. How do we know they will listen to us this time? No one has listened to us all day."

"Well, except Laz, but I get your point," Lucia slumped right in the spot she was in, "So, what do we do?" Lucia went deep into thought, almost like she was meditating.

"I know! Let's go!" they restarted their race and bounded through the desert sand. They were so close they could almost smell their freedom, both their parents and their "bodies" were facing away from them, looking at the picturesque sunset. Well, Cleo and Caesar were rolling in the sand in Izzy's and Lucia's bodies and licking their limbs, then being distracted and looking at the Sun, then starting again.

Izzy and Lucia were so close to their dad that he felt their whiskers on his leg.

He suddenly jumped around. "Cleo, Caesar??" He exclaimed, his face full of confusion.

"Dad!"

CHAPTER: 12

"Dad, Dad, it's us," Izzy screeched in her loudest voice, but all that came out were the cute whimpers of a meow from Cleo's body. While she was pulling her paws up at Paul's legs, trying in any way to get his attention, Lucia had disappeared. When Izzy turned around, feeling rejected yet again, Lucia was nowhere to be seen.

"Paul, am I going mad, or is that Cleo?"

"It looks so much like her," Paul replied, "but how did she get here?"

"Let me look at her... yes, that's her for sure."

Paul scooped Izzy up in his arms. Izzy felt a huge breeze of warmth like a blanket was pulled around her body. It felt amazing to be reunited with her dad, even if she was still nuzzling into him with her cat face and tickling him with her blotchy cat tail.

"Wait, hang on, is that Caesar over there??"

"You're joking, aren't you?" One of Paul's favourite phrases, but it was no joke, Caesar, aka Lucia was heading in their direction.

"Why has he got a stick in his mouth?" Both adults were bemused by the whole situation. Their family pets were in the middle of the desert. Their kids were acting crazy by licking each other and sniffing their bums. Their cats were the noisiest they'd ever been. They felt they needed to go home and have a strong drink of grape juice (wink wink).

"Look, what is he doing?" Paul pointed with his free hand at the ginger stripy cat with the stick in his mouth. The sand was moving under the stick as Lucia's mouth moved left and right with urgency, and it began to look like some sort of message.

"What are you doing, Lucia?" Izzy was just as confused as her parents (well, maybe not AS confused as them; she knew more than them, but she had no idea what Lucia was doing now).

"Mhmmh mhmh." Lucia didn't drop the stick and continued to move it around in the sand. It began to spell out a group of letters.

I   AM   Lu-

"Look, it's a message."

I   AM   Lucia   MY BODY SWITCHED seesar

I know, I can't really spell Caesar. I mean, I am only seven! And I've never seen the 'ee' sound with an ae before.

Both adults looked as shocked as someone who had just let out a thunderous fart in an elevator when they thought it would be a silent but violent one.

Their eyes were bulging out of their faces in amazement. Paul stumbled back, dropping Izzy. Luckily, her cat skills allowed her to transform the fall into a leap, and she landed safely and gracefully on all four feet. Both Izzy and Lucia sat by their human bodies and used their paws to point at them to continue to get their parents to comprehend what had happened.

"Wait, what?" Paul wiped the sweat forming on his brow, "You two are..." he pointed at Izzy and Lucia's bodies, which were now sitting on the floor in a Heron Pose, licking their legs. Now, if you don't know a Heron pose, Google it. If you don't want to put the book down or are not allowed on the Internet, I'll try, and describe it. Heron Pose is when you sit on your bottom and put one leg up straight as close to your head as you can. Apparently, it is good for flexibility, but I have no idea why it is called a Heron pose when a Heron is a bird and birds do not put their legs close to their heads.

There's been a cat, girl, sister switch." Once the girls' parents had time to process what was happening - with a lot of staring and mumbling and gulping like a fish. They stepped into action. Kids often moan about their parents and sigh when they ask them to clean their rooms, but one thing they will do without any explanation is try to save their lives, and this is what Izzy and Lucia's parents did. They scooped up both cats (still Izzy and Lucia). Paul grabbed Cleo and Caesar's hands and dragged them to the car.

As Izzy and Lucia were being jumbled up and down being carried to the car, Izzy was in awe of Lucia.

"That was amazing, Lucia," she stuttered while being rushed to the car, "focused writing to the max!" Lucia beamed inside and out while they were being thrown into the car with haste, and Paul was forcing Cleo and Caesar into the back seats.

The car zoomed away from the desert, bumping up and down like a rollercoaster. Izzy and Lucia sat together on their mum's lap. She held onto them with a tight grip as their dad swerved through the bustling Dubai traffic.

'We need to figure out how to switch back,' Izzy purred to Lucia, 'what is the last thing you can remember last night?'

'I don't know, Izzy, I really can't remember.'

'Lucia, try to focus, really think back. Take a deep breath and imagine you are in your room, in your body.' Lucia let her mind drift back to that night. She ignored the memories of her toys that she had left sprayed out across the floor, she disregarded her stomach, which was grumbling for food (for some reason, Bagel had popped into her mind. There! She was there in her imagination. She was in her room, lying on her bed next to Caesar, feeling annoyed with her dad. 'If we were Cleo and Caesar, it would be easy.' Lucia's eyes began to flutter asleep as a huge bolt of lightning illuminated the villa.

'That's it!'

'OW!!' In Lucia's excitement, she dug her claws into her mum's lap.

'There was lightning. That's what caused the switch, but how do we switch back? You know what it's like in Dubai. We won't have another storm in ages, maybe even a year!' Lucia's amber, glowing eyes widened in dismay.

'Wait.' Izzy's tail started swishing, 'you're right, this is Dubai. If we don't get real lightning, what's the next best thing?' Lucia looked at her, confused.

'A light show!'

Then, in unison, the lightbulbs sparked into action, 'WE NEED TO GET TO DUBAI MALL.'

CHAPTER: 13

Inside the car, different emotions were bouncing around the seats: worry, excitement, confusion, fear. But on the outside, the car rolled to a halt at the red traffic light. Paul held his shaking foot on the brake as he kept looking at the rear-view mirror, staring at his children, who were his cats.

'Only one problem, Lucia, how do we get Dad to turn the car around? We are nearly at home.'

Now, it was Izzy's turn to problem-solve. She began pawing at her mum's pocket, which had her phone in.

'You need this?' Her mum looked confused, but she quickly unlocked the phone and lent it to Izzy so she could use it. Izzy used her nose to open Wazes and very slowly (with a few typos) pressed the directions to Dubai Mall. Since going on Noon Food, she had become a pro at using a phone as a cat. She thought she might train Cleo and Caesar to try and use a phone to communicate with them if they ever got out of this mess.

'Paul, we've got to go to Dubai Mall.' As soon as the lights turned green, Paul twisted the steering wheel into the far-left lane to take the U-turn. The sounds of beeping and screeching of wheels filled the night sky.

Dad's driving is usually really good. *Except when he has House music on, and he's hitting the steering wheel to the music, then he gets a bit "swervy".*

Yes, but at least he's better than Mum. *Agreed!* **But she does say that her parallel parking is something to be proud of.** *I don't really know what parallel parking is but whenever she manages it, she gives herself a little cheer so it must be tricky.* **When I drive, I'm going to be better than both mum and dad.** *Me too.*

They arrived at the Dubai Mall entrance just as dusk metamorphosised into night. Unfortunately, this was when everyone else decided to arrive at Dubai Mall, too. The family suddenly hit the usual evening traffic. The Collins loved living in Dubai. The only problem was, so did a lot of other people, which inevitably equals traffic. Each car was bumper to bumper as the only sounds from outside were the revving of engines and the distant beeping of horns from someone who had cut in the line at the last minute. The exhaust smoke drifted as high as the glimmering moon as the city lights began to twinkle. Each car offered its own mini story.

In one car, you could see a young woman loving the songs on the radio a little bit too much. Her eyes were closed, singing at the top of her voice to the ballade being blared out the speakers. She remembered the last karaoke night she had with her friends at Lucky Voice, where she bellowed out the same song and got the crowd roaring. In another car, there was a slightly different sort of blaring. This blaring was from a couple, well they were arguing like a couple, shouting and screaming at each other. The roaring from the car was causing the teenager in the back to roll his eyes and put his airpods in. Spit from the argument, flew around the car. My guess is that the driver took the wrong turn, and he blamed the passenger for their directions. Classic car argument. Another car further back was filled with excited friends all dressed up. Each person was talking over one another and laughed at their own jokes. Every two seconds, there was a flash, as a selfie was taken for Insta. Each car trundled along with their stories, but my guess is that the Collins story was by far the most interesting of that night. Two children turned into cats, and two cats turned into children. Yes, definitely, wins the most exciting story from the car traffic jam.

Finally, after a loud meow from Izzy, Paul halted abruptly and pulled into the only parking spot left on Level 7. The whole family took one huge sigh, even the cats.

Dad doesn't parallel park, he's all about the reverse parking.

'Right, now what?' asked their mum. Izzy knew what they had to do but knew it was going to be the most dangerous thing she (or probably anyone in her family) had done in her life, and what's worse, Lucia had to do it, too. Paul ran around each door, letting out cats, children, and his wife (best to open every door at this point). The adults let the cats lead the way from the car park. It was clear that they had all the answers and the parents had none - this was not something they were used to. They raced into the mall, and the glare of the lights reflected from the cat's tapetum lucidum.

MUM, what have we told you? No one wants to know about the reflective part at the back of a cat's eye that helps them see if it's dark. It's not a science lesson.

Each shop was like an amusement park, with lights flashing and rows of colourful displays. I mean, you don't become the largest mall in the world by looking boring. They rushed past the ice rink (yes, an ice rink in the desert), past the fountains, past the prehistoric dinosaur model and towards the aquarium. Izzy, Lucia, Cleo and Caesar stopped. Frozen still by the view in front of them. Their necks craned upwards at the pulsating kaleidoscope of colours in the liquid window. Sharks, stingrays, and fish swam past as the water currents flowed. Izzy and Lucia were beginning to pick up cat instincts and were mesmerised by the aquatic display in front of them. Cleo and Caesar still had their cat instincts intact and stumbled towards the glass, wanting to chase the immense fish in the glitzy water.

"Come on, you guys, we need to stay focused, we are causing a scene" Their mum ushered them forward. She was right, people were starting to stare and all they needed was another security guard throwing them onto the street. Izzy and Lucia snapped back into action and galloped past the aquarium, taking one longing look back at the fish dancing in the underwater tunnel.

They finally raced through Fashion Avenue and reached the entrance to the Burj Khalifa. They stared upwards at the shimmering exterior. The Burj Khalifa is the tallest building in the world and is a spectacle in the middle of the desert. As they all caught their breaths, cats panting, humans sweating, Izzy turned to Lucia.

"I have a plan, but it's dangerous. Really dangerous." Izzy paused for dramatic tension. Even though she was in a precarious situation, she could still add the melodrama of a pre-teen to her conversation. "You know, every night, there is a light show projected onto the Burj Khalifa."

"Yes, we've seen it a million times, why?"

"Well, this is similar to lightning hitting our villa, right, a light 'lighting' up a building. Get it?"

"But that means," Lucia started.

"Yep." Izzy said, "We need to go up!"

CHAPTER: 14

Luckily, Izzy had learned about structures in Grade 2. When she was researching the Burj Khalifa, she found out that they had installed tiny spotlights to make the outside look 3D. So basically, there are 1.2 million LED lights attached to the 828-metre tower, not many, eh?

Izzy pointed to her mum's phone in her pocket. She unlocked the screen and passed it to Izzy. Painstakingly, Izzy typed the very basic instructions to her parents.

Find the laptop and make it lightning.

Coincidentally, as their mum was also a teacher at their school and had taught in Grade 2, she knew exactly what Izzy meant. She grabbed Paul's hand and rushed him back into the mall, puzzlement rippling through his body. He was meant to have listened to Izzy present her PowerPoint, but there was 'a big game' on that night, so he had what's called half listened (which is parent code for not listened at all). As they disappeared, Izzy turned to Lucia.

'Lucia, we have to do this on our own. Well, with Cleo and Caesar, are you with me?'

'Always.' They both jumped up and hit the elevator arrow pointing up. As the elevator opened, Izzy and Lucia nudged Cleo and Caesar into the small box. They whooshed upwards towards the 148th floor. As they got higher and higher, their ears began to pop, and their stomachs fluttered with dread. Even though the Burj Khalifa lift is incredibly fast, it felt like a snail's pace to Izzy and Lucia who were trying to get their lives back.

"Where have Mum and Dad gone?" Lucia asked.

"Well, when me and Mum were researching the Burj Khalifa, we found out that a computer programme controls what image is on the light show of the Burj Khalifa, so they have gone to find the laptop to change the programme to a lightning bolt. Once this changes, we will have recreated last night... well, that's the plan."

Even as a cat, you could see the nerves across Izzy's face.

"So, what do we need to do?"

Izzy hung her head and couldn't bring herself to say the words. She sat at the feet of her own body. Cleo was using Izzy's hands to scratch her ears, and her human eyes darted around the elevator, feeling trapped. Caesar was also twitchy and kept using Lucia's feet to walk around the microscopic space back and forth, back and forth, until Lucia used her cat body to stretch out as much as she could to stop him from walking.

After what felt like an eternity, the ding of the elevator rang through everyone's ears like a siren. Izzy and Lucia stepped out onto the observation deck, and their jaws fell to the floor (just like in cartoons when characters are really shocked). They had never been up so high before.

They were 828 metres above the ground. EIGHT HUNDRED, not eight. EIGHT HUNDRED metres from standing on the ground where thousands of people were doing their shopping below them. At night, the view was quite spectacular. They could see miles around, and each skyscraper glimmered in the darkness. Each car was like a tiny, iridescent ant crawling along the road.

Both Izzy and Lucia took a huge gulp. Cleo and Caesar stood frozen in the elevator, and it took Izzy and Lucia to use their claws to 'convince' their human bodies to come out. The wind whipped around their faces, and they felt their blood freeze as fear took over. They crept to the edge of the observation deck, avoiding the security guards, and peered over the edge.

Izzy was imagining her mum and dad rushing around the room in the secret parts that nobody usually goes to. Darting around the brick corridors to the launch room where the laptop will be. Izzy dreamed it would be sitting like a treasure chest, shining at her mum ready to put the code in. In reality, it was in a small box-shaped grey room alongside a million other pieces of technical equipment. Paul and their mum had their work cut out to change the light show to lightning but they were as determined as their girls to get their children back.

"Remind me again how we are going to get close to the lights," quivered Lucia, looking for a different answer from Izzy to the one she knew she was going to say.

"About that, so we need to get as close to the lights as we can." Izzy took another gulp while she peered over the edge. "At the moment, we are far away from the lights..."

"The only way to get closer is..." Lucia looked again at her sister.

Izzy and Lucia whispered in unison, "We have to go over!"

They both looked at each other with dread and trust. Looking down had made the situation a million times worse as they now knew how far down they would fall if this went wrong.

'When Mum has changed the light show, we have to go over the observation deck with Cleo and Caesar, and we should switch back.' Izzy explained, her canines chattering.

'And if we don't change back?' Lucia could barely get her voice out and made the smallest meow sound.

'Then we keep falling towards the fountains at the bottom.'

'The fountains that are 828 metres down? Those fountains??' Again, Lucia knew the answer but couldn't bear to think of the deadly consequences.

The girls waited patiently for the National colours being displayed on the Burj Khalifa to turn to the recognisable lightning bolt light show. As they waited, they put their paws together, knowing having a sister was the hardest and the very best thing ever.

I one hundred per cent agree. *I, one million per cent, agree!* **The very best.** *Aww thanks Izzy, are you getting emotional because this part of the story is really worrying and scary.* **NO! I mean no. I mean, okay yes...**

Out of the corner of their cat crescent eyes, they saw the green luminous lights transform into an electrifying show of a lightning storm.

'After three,' the girls jumped onto Cleo and Caesar's human backs, 'two,' they dug their claws in to get the two humans to jump forward, 'one.' All four of them launched themselves off the tallest building in the world, plummeting down to the ground....

CHAPTER: 15

"Do you need another tissue?" Paul walked into the living room and passed Izzy and Lucia's mum another box of tissues. She had cried so much her nose was red and blotchy.

"Thanks," her eyes were rimmed in a bright red colour as tears welled up, ready to gush out. "I just can't cope, Paul,"

"You're such a wimp, Mum." Lucia jumped onto the sofa and gave her mum a huge, human-style hug, "It's just a film, and you've seen it so many times before."

You didn't think we would really not survive, did you? *That would have been so dark! Let's rewind to last night to explain a few things...*

"AARRRRGGGGHHHHHH!" The girls and the cats all screamed as they plummeted down the colossal Burj Khalifa tower. Getting faster and faster, their hopes of surviving were disappearing as rapidly as their speed. All of a sudden, Izzy caught a glimpse of her paw, which was no longer a paw; it was a human hand being held in front of her. Lucia looked around to see her ginger tail but found only her bottom sticking out behind her.

HEY!! **Lucia** *it doesn't matter, you had clothes on, how we managed to get our clothes back on I have no idea. Yes* **Izzy,** *that's the unbelievable part?!*

As they got closer to the floor, they miraculously slowed down. Izzy could see Cleo, her wonderful, beautiful cat, in front of her. Her black, brown and white fur coat danced in the breeze. Lucia could see Caesar, her cheeky, mischievous cat next to her, his ginger, stripy tail waving in the wind. By the time they got to the ground floor, they were practically floating, and they all phenomenally landed on their feet, though moments later fell to the floor in shock over what had just happened. I mean, they had just travelled 828 metres down. That would surprise anybody a little bit. Hopefully, if you have learned anything from this book, you now know the Burj Khalifa is… wait for it… 828 metres tall!

Their parents slammed open the fire exit and rushed over to all of them. Instinctively, they hugged the girls, then held them at arm's length.

"Izzy?" Paul looked deep into her eyes to see if he could recognise his firstborn child.

"Lucia?" The girl's mum just knew that her babies were back in the correct body. Cleo and Caesar purred and fussed around everyone's legs in the only way cats can.

"Mum, Dad? Can we go home? We've had a pretty crazy day."

EPILOGUE

So that's our story. I won't tell you which bits were made up, but they might not be the parts you expect. *I'll give you a clue: there are no stray cats in the Metro. They are so super clean that there would be nothing for them to eat.* Anyway, Mum said she needed to include an Epilogue or something. *What's that?* It's the part of the story that everyone always skips before they give the book back to Mrs Green (she's our librarian, and although she's really cool, you don't mess with her library system. You HAVE to give your book back on the right day or you get an email to your parents). *Mum said she never reads those emails anyway because the book is usually stuffed under Izzy's bed or somewhere else in the house. As she's made the effort to write it, I suppose we should let her get on with it.*

As Paul started the engine of the car and reversed out of the drive, he noticed an orange glint in his rearview mirror. "Caesar, not today!" he spotted Caesar clambering on the top of his car's roof and began chilling like a ninja. Cleo hopped up to join him as the car rolled backwards.

"Look, Izzy, the cats want to come with us!" Lucia was cackling, pointing out her window, and Izzy squeezed her hand with a big smile on her face.

"Right, guys, not this time. Humans only today, we have got two pick-ups to do on the way." Izzy and Lucia's mum jumped out of the car and tried her hardest to usher the cats down (which ended up being another comedy show for Lucia as their mum wasn't very tall and the cats had no intention of going anywhere). Finally, after everyone got out of the car and helped, the cats were put back in the house, and the door was firmly closed. They began their weekend journey through the Dubai traffic.

All four girls clambered out of the car in the stifling car park still chattering away about random drama at school, someone had called Lucia a peabrain and Izzy was not happy about it. Paul had one of those cars that had seats in the 'backback' that you had to do some sort of torturous gymnastics to get out of. Finally, everyone was out of the car and wiped their brows, wondering why Izzy and Lucia had chosen this venue in the middle of summer.

Once Izzy and Lucia had returned to their original bodies, everything went back to normal, apart from a few small changes. Izzy worked with Fatima to do her maths homework and was actually better at problem-solving than her friend, though she did need some help with the seven times tables! Lucia decided to take the inquiry station seat in her classroom. This was a table where you could sit alone and complete your work independently. I mean, she didn't sit there all the time. Sometimes, she liked to return to her old seat where she could see the nearly finished building being constructed. They still both went to break on the magic floating playground; just this time, when they saw each other, they would give each other a huge hug and then join their friends. (I did catch them doing this once, and my heart exploded!).

"You know, I was thinking," Izzy said to Lucia before she lined up for Spanish, "it wasn't so bad being a cat for a day."

What? You wanted to get things back to normal as soon as possible," Lucia whispered.

"I know, but now we know how to turn back. It could be useful one day,"

"I like your thinking, Izzy," and with that, Lucia trotted to join her friends on the playground as Mr Baldy ushered Izzy to the line with his arms folded across his wide chest.

Anyway, back to the day out, Izzy had invited Fatima, and Lucia had invited Liliana to come to the Creek for a special dessert.

"Why have we come here?" Fatima could feel her dark hair beginning to frizz, "couldn't we have stayed by the pool today?"

"Sorry." Izzy strolled arm in arm with Fatima and her sister. "Lucia and I have something we need to do."

As the group arrived at a little café with blue and white tiles on the inside, they sat at a rather too small black table. Paul took a piece of card and folded it to put under one of the rusty old legs to stop it wobbling; Lucia took the order.

"Can we order 2 coffees, one Fattoush salad and an extra dessert? But we need to pay for 2!" Paul spat his iced coffee out over the table.

"Sorry, Dad," the girls said in unison, "we owe them!"

www.ingramcontent.com/pod-product-compliance
Lightning Source LLC
LaVergne TN
LVHW021122080426
835513LV00011B/1198